Authentic Designs from the American Arts and Crafts Movement

Selected from *Keramic Studio*

Edited by Carol Belanger Grafton

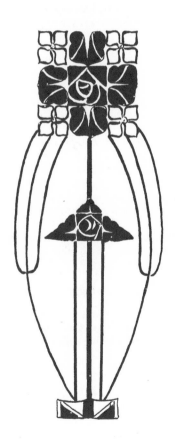

Dover Publications, Inc., *New York*

Authentic Designs from the American Arts and Crafts Movement: Selected from "Keramic Studio" is a new work, first published by Dover Publications, Inc., in 1988.

DOVER *Pictorial Archive* SERIES

This book belongs to the Dover Pictorial Archive Series. You may use the designs and illustrations for graphics and crafts applications, free and without special permission, provided that you include no more than ten in the same publication or project. For permission for additional use, please email the Permissions Department at rights@doverpublications.com or write to Dover Publications, Inc., 31 East 2nd Street, Mineola, New York 11501.

However, resale, licensing, republication, reproduction or distribution of any illustration by any other graphic service, whether it be in a book or in any other design resource, is strictly prohibited.

Library of Congress Cataloging-in-Publication Data

Authentic designs from the American arts and crafts movement / selected from Keramic studio ; edited by Carol Belanger Grafton.
      p.   cm.—(Dover pictorial archive series)
    Includes index.
    ISBN-13: 978-0-486-25800-3 (pbk.)
    ISBN-10: 0-486-25800-9 (pbk.)
    1. Arts and crafts movement—United States—Themes, motives. 2. Pottery, American—Themes, motives. I. Grafton, Carol Belanger. II. Keramic studio. III. Series.
NK1403.7.A98 1988
745.4'4973–dc19
                                          88-16201
                                          CIP

Manufactured in the United States by LSC Communications
4500053990
www.doverpublications.com

⌘ Publisher's Note

The second half of the nineteenth century in Europe saw a flowering of decorative arts in reaction to what was seen as a decline in taste and craftsmanship brought about by mass production. This renewed interest in craftsmanship and design manifested itself in the Arts and Crafts Movement, which developed in England in the 1860s. Led by the poet and designer William Morris, the movement stressed a return to the principles of craftsmanship as practiced in the Middle Ages, and brought about a revival in the production of handcrafted jewelry, wallpaper, textiles, books and decorative metalwork.

By the 1890s the Arts and Crafts Movement tended to merge with the ornamental style known as Art Nouveau, which flourished in Europe and the United States from about 1890 to 1910 and influenced not only the crafts, such as ceramics, jewelry and glasswork, but architecture, interior design, posters and illustration as well. This fresh manifestation grew out of a deliberate attempt to create a new style free of the imitative historicism that characterized much of nineteenth-century art. It has been seen as an outgrowth of the "linearism" evident in the drawings of William Blake and Aubrey Beardsley in England, and the work of Gauguin and Toulouse-Lautrec in France, while the current interest in Japanese prints was also an influence.

It was out of this union of the Arts and Crafts Movement and the Art Nouveau style that *Keramic Studio* was born. Founded in 1899 and published for over twenty-five years by the ceramicist Adelaide Alsop Robineau (1865–1929) and her husband Samuel Robineau, the magazine carried designs and patterns that could be used in painting porcelain, as well as articles by ceramic experts such as Charles Volkmar, Taxile Doat, Charles Binns and Frederick H. Rhead. Directed at first to the serious amateur, the publication later added articles of a more technical nature. Together with the Arts and Crafts school established by Mrs. Robineau at Four Winds, her home in Syracuse, *Keramic Studio* made an important contribution to early twentieth-century ceramics, while the work of its founder was sold by Tiffany and Company and exhibited both in the United States and abroad.

The designs in this book are authentic examples selected and arranged by Carol Belanger Grafton from *Keramic Studio* Volumes 8–22 and 24–29 (May 1906–April 1928) and representing the work of over a hundred artists. In the material from the earlier years, the characteristics of the Art Nouveau style are amply illustrated by the emphasis on sinuous line and movement, lyrically abstracted natural forms and a flowing repetition of stylized motifs. But the present selection, extending as it does over a number of years, also exhibits such other influences as Wiener Werkstätte and early Art Deco. An amazing variety of structurally accurate yet streamlined flowers, plants, birds, and even insects adorn the borders of plates and bowls, while geometric shapes take on a new life, combining and intersecting in intricate patterns. The use of cut-out shapes and the interplay of positive and negative space suggest an emphasis on light and dark; yet the colors used often tended toward earth tones and involved subtle contrasts.

Artists and craftsmen will find this collection an invaluable source of ideas for designs in this popular style, either for direct use or for adaptation to a variety of applications in many areas other than ceramics. For the art historian, an alphabetical list of artists is provided, giving the page numbers on which their work appears. For those who wish to work from the object to the artist, the small number alongside any drawing with an identified artist is keyed to the number preceding the artist's name in the alphabetical list. It will be observed that the overwhelming majority of artists included are women.

⊞ Alphabetical List of Artists Represented

*May Warner and May Warner Cole are probably the same.

*This design was entered in a competition under the name of Rosedale, but the name of the designer was lost.

*May Warner and May Warner Cole are probably the same.

22

5

1

99

93

2

84

84

84

119

64

116

116

116

116

113

113

113

119

4

119

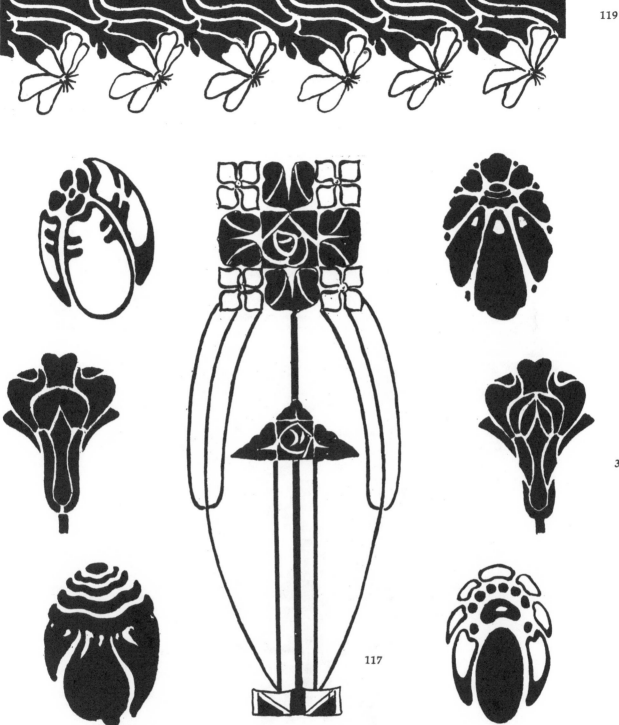

3

3

117

119

5

48

111

7

57

6

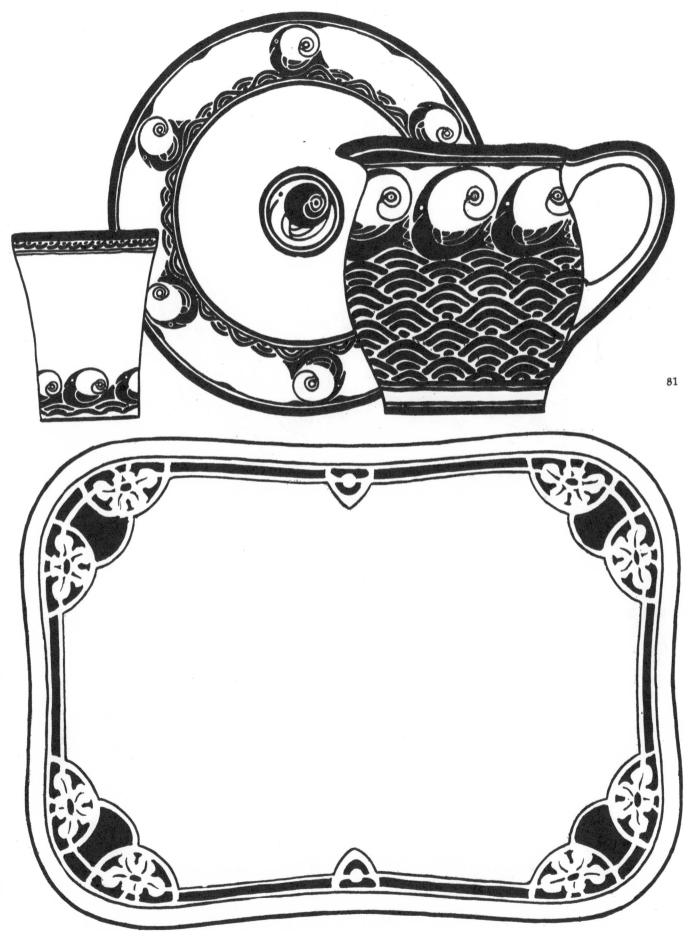

81

7

15

44

8

15

15

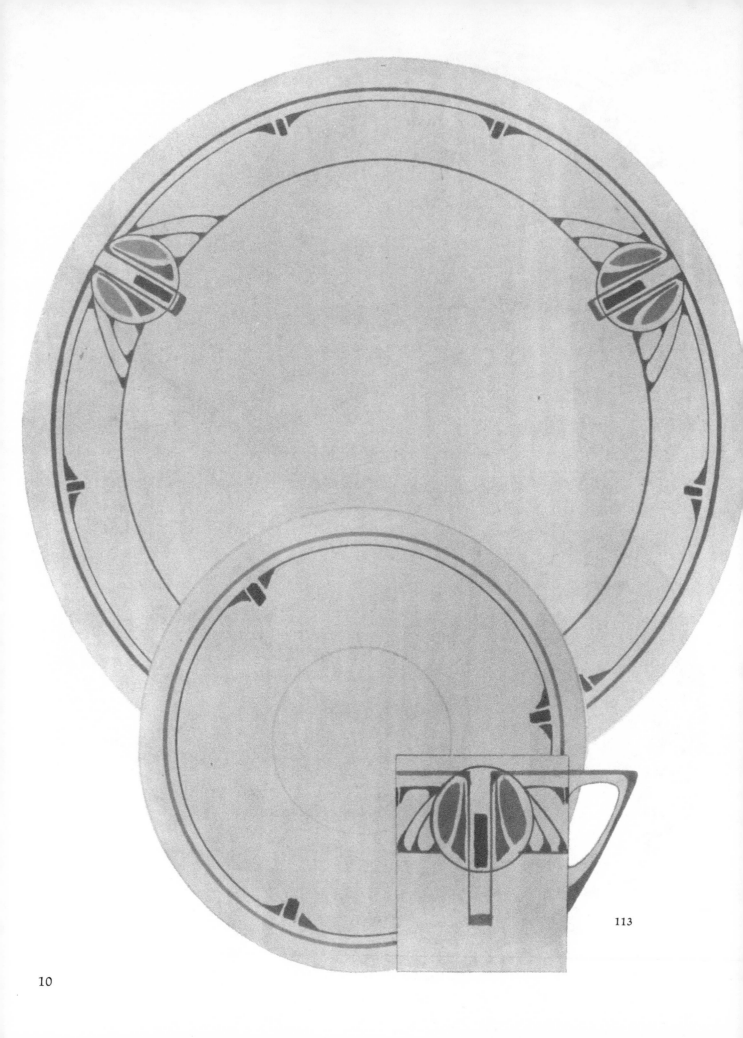

42

42

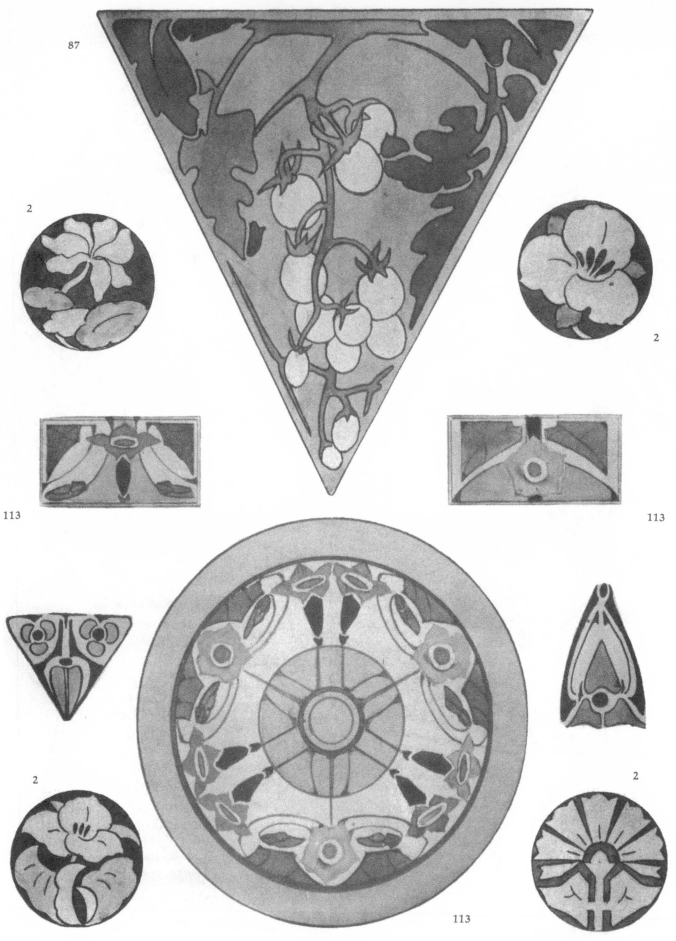

87

2

2

113

113

2

2

113

12

62

62

62

13

47

14

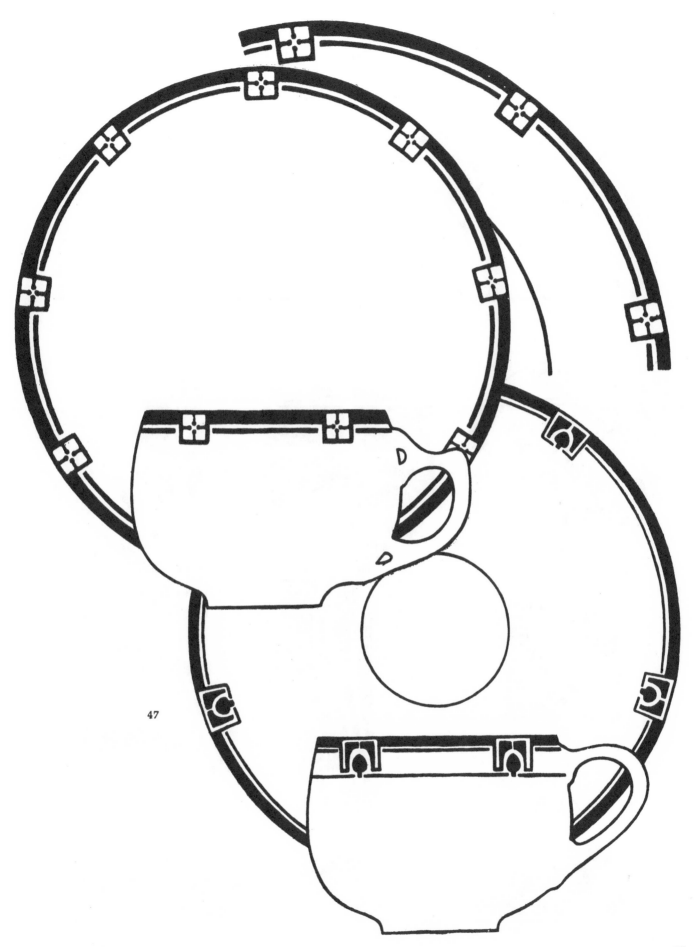

47

16

64

3

113

113

47

64

47

83

36

17

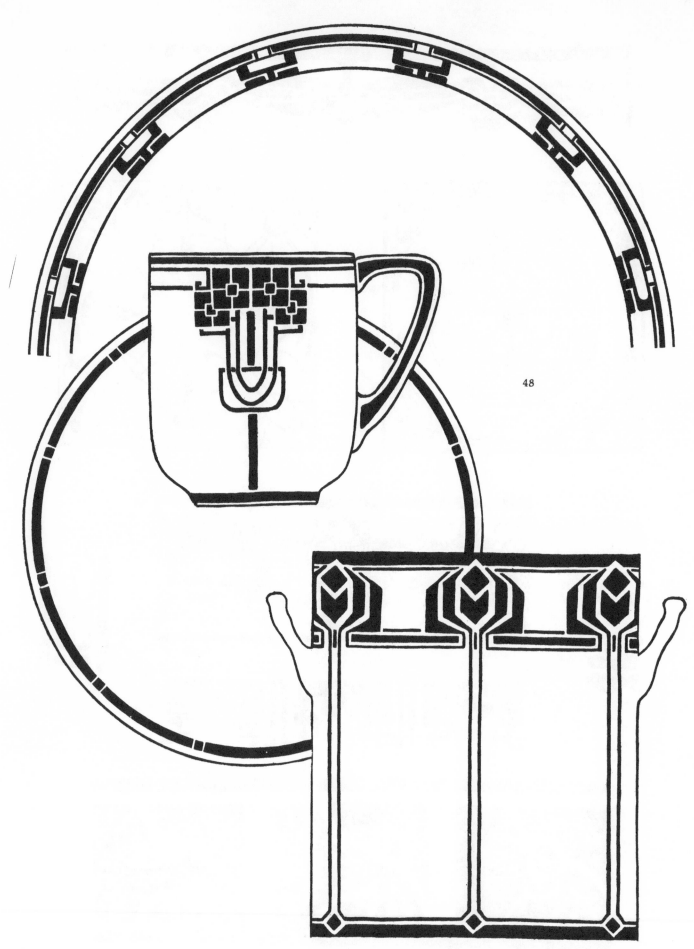

48

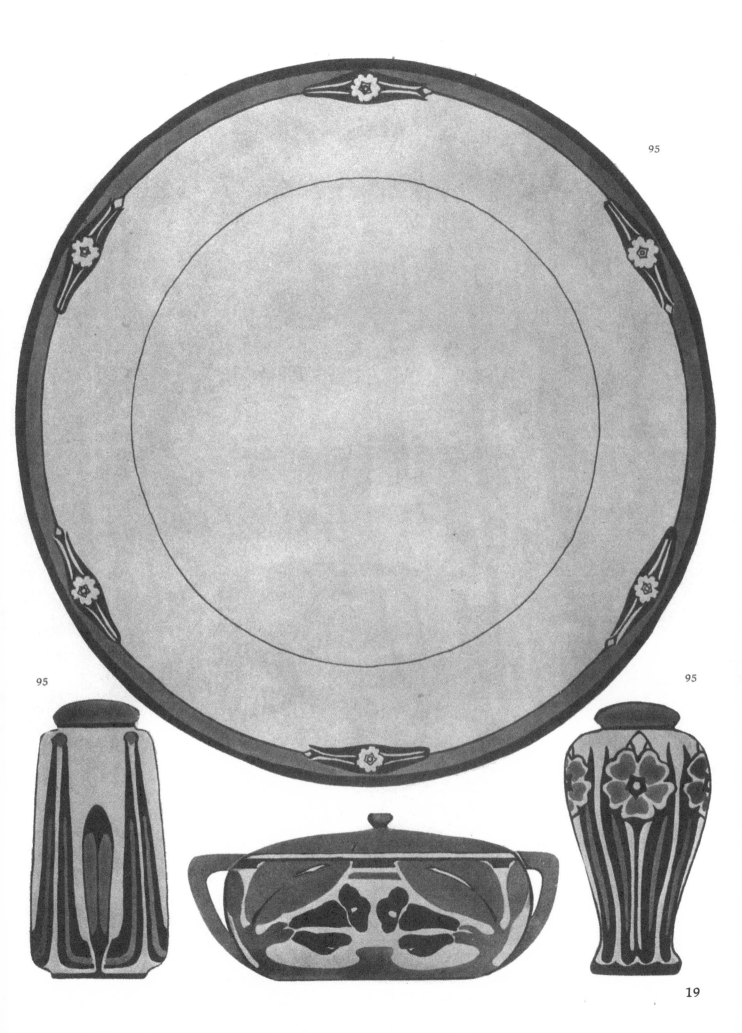

95

95   95

19

84

84

84

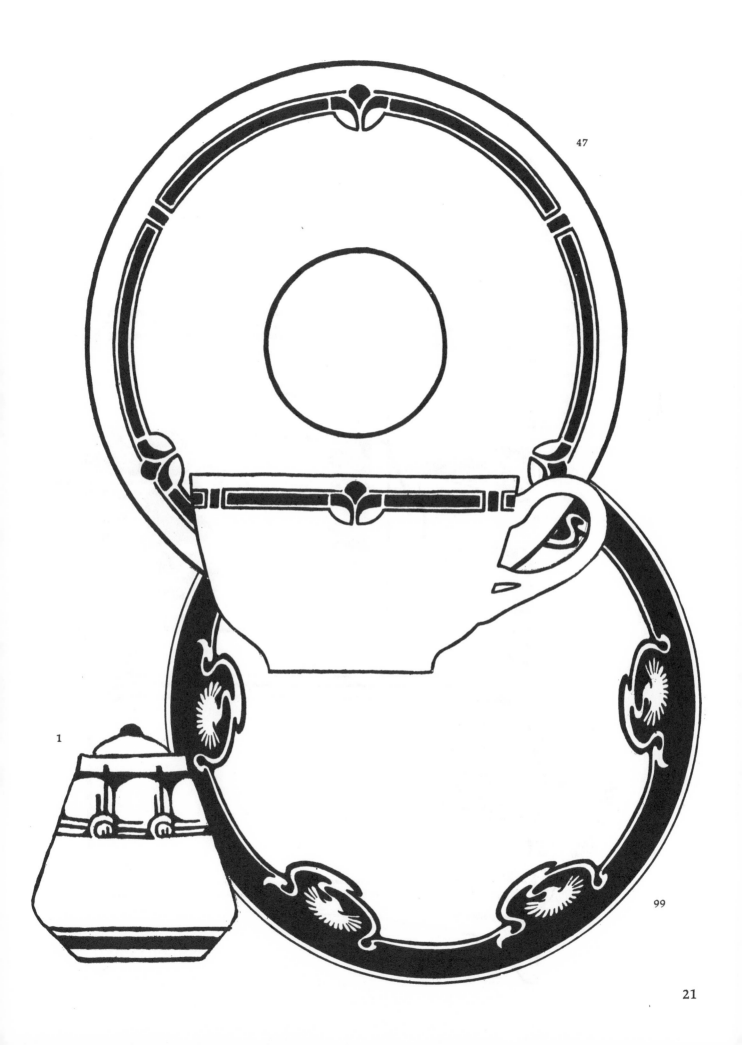

47

1

99

21

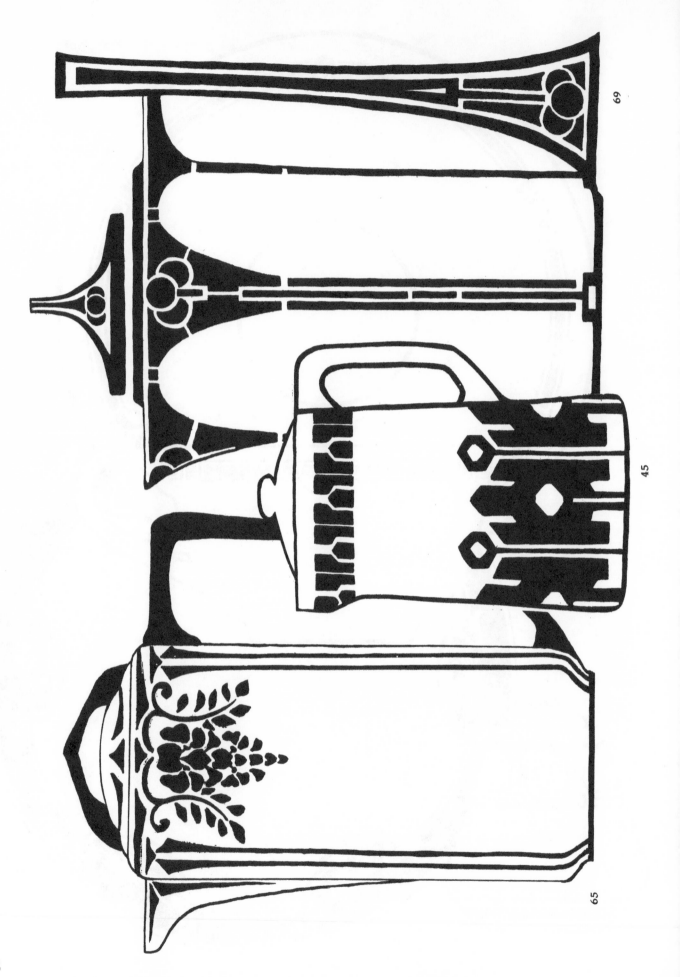

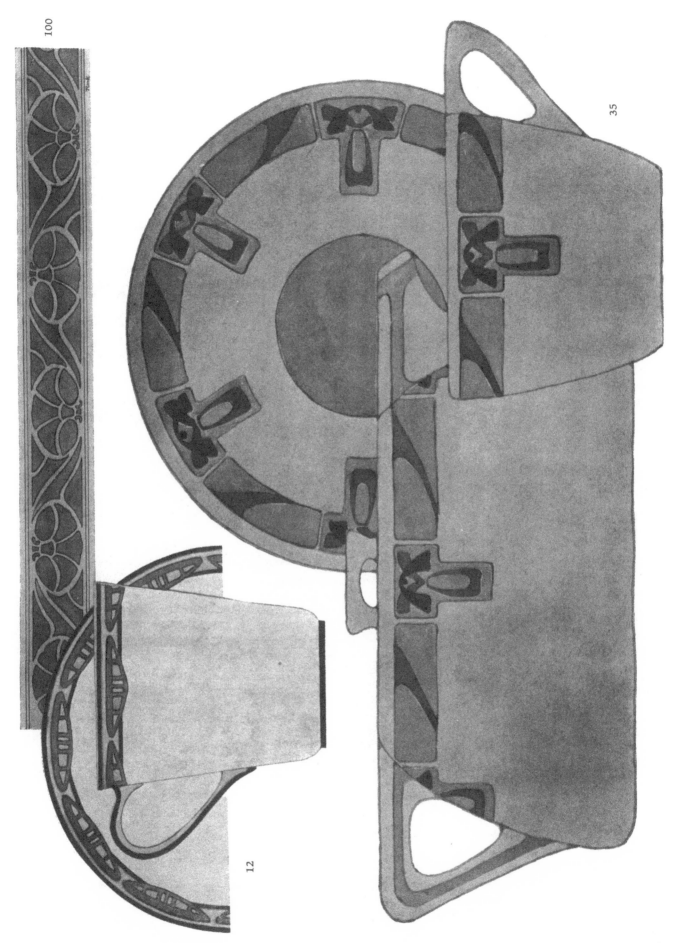

100

35

12

23

114

91

24

94

32

42

56

39

30

26

44

50

Lena E. Hanssen
1914

78

27

42

110

89

17

47

47

47

88

88

88

88

16

47

88

105

116

32

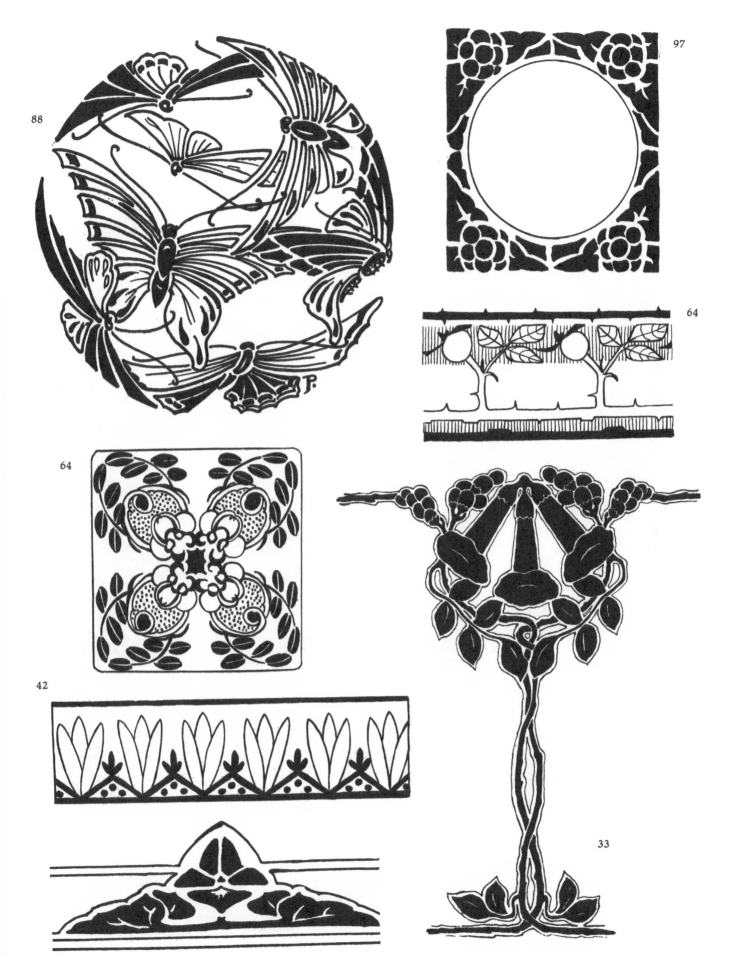

88

97

64

64

42

33

33

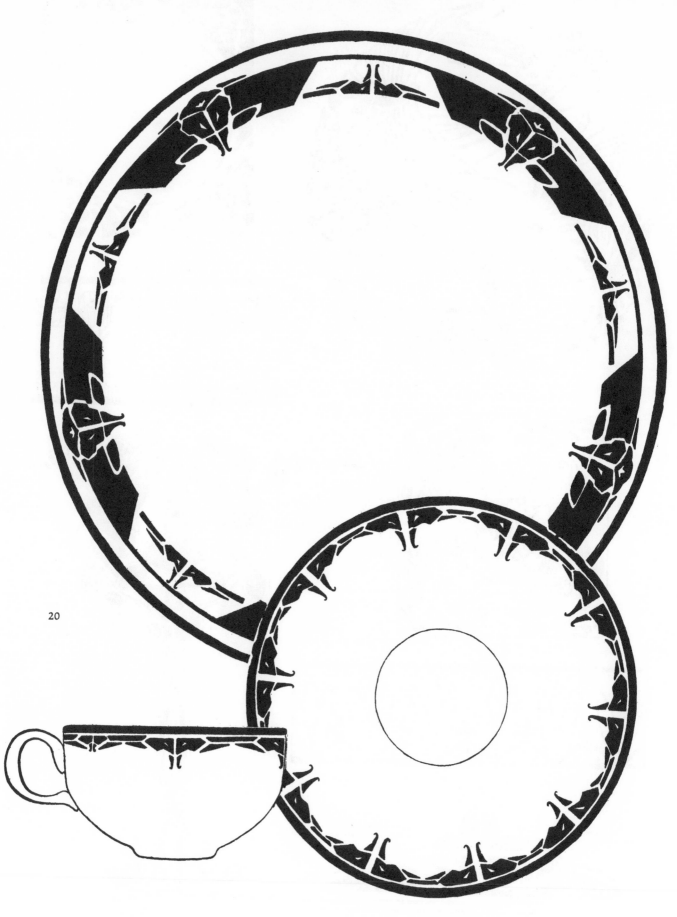

20

34

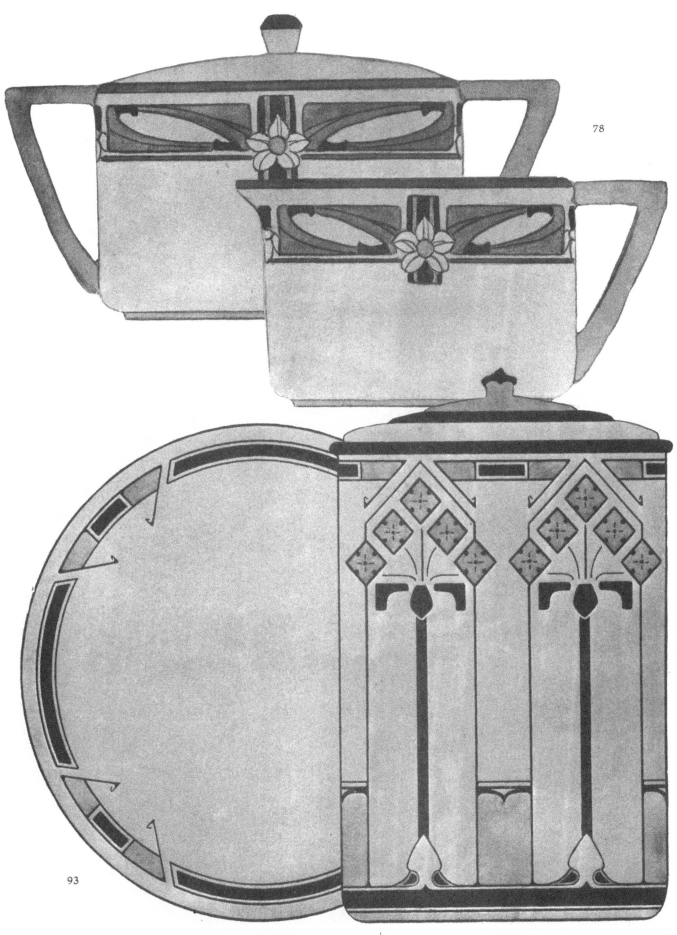

78

93

35

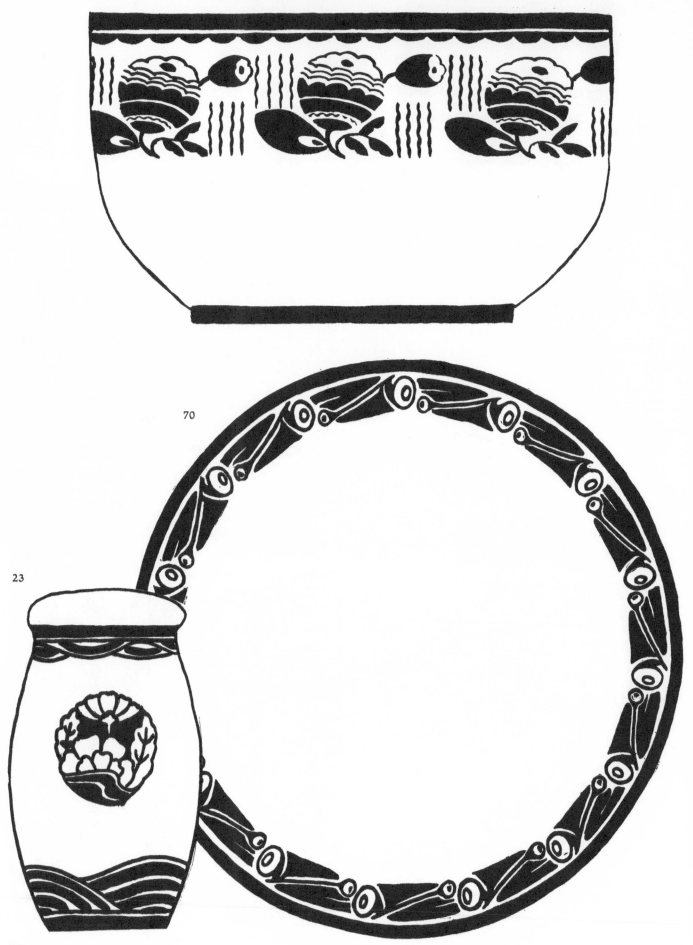

70

23

36

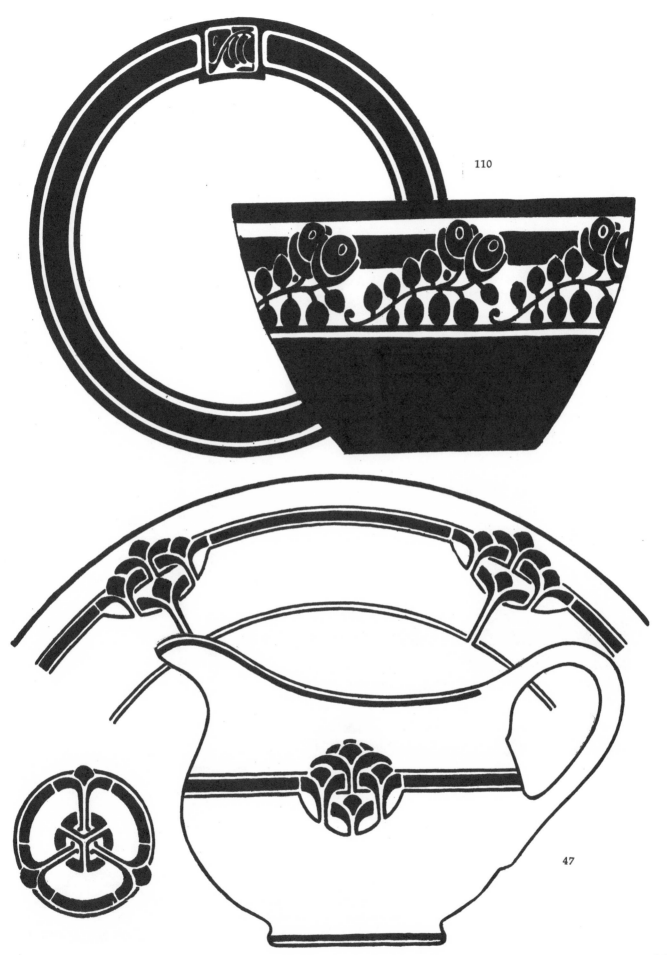

110

47

2

80

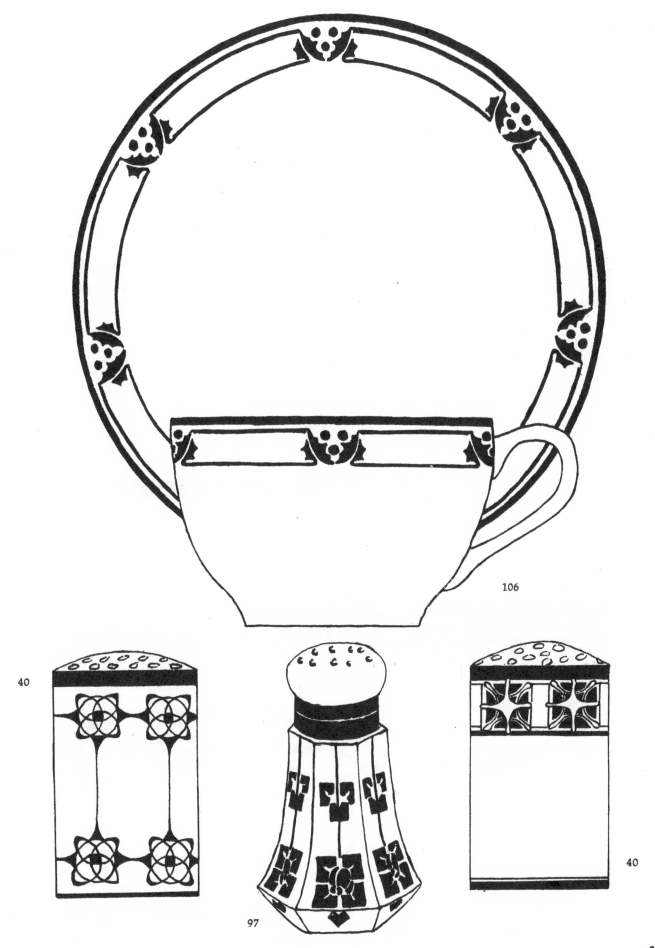

106

40

97

40

39

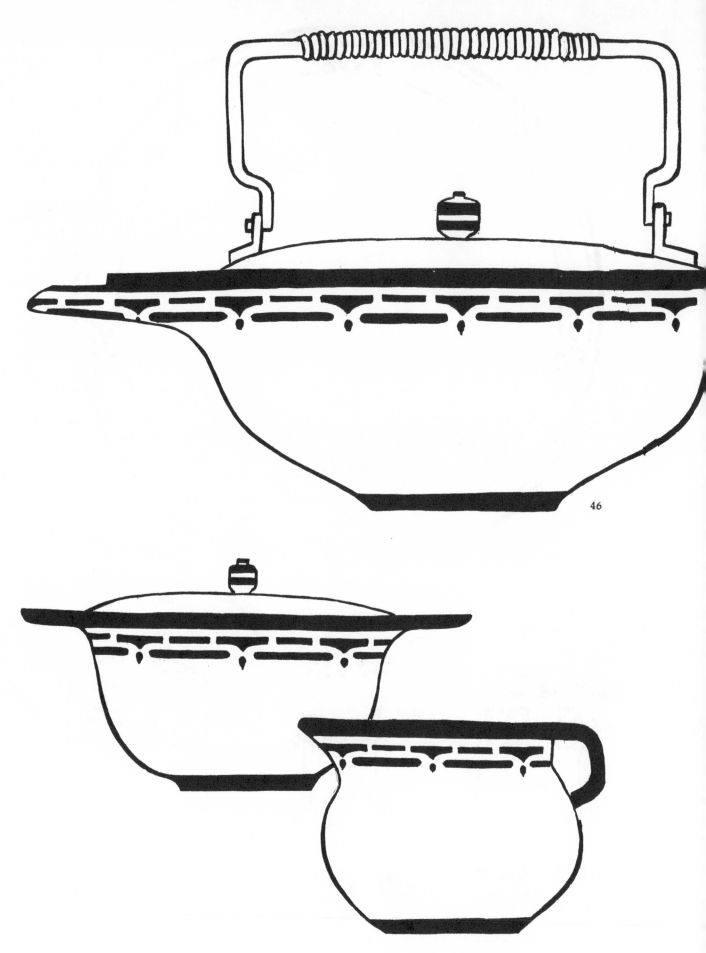

46

115

28

104

41

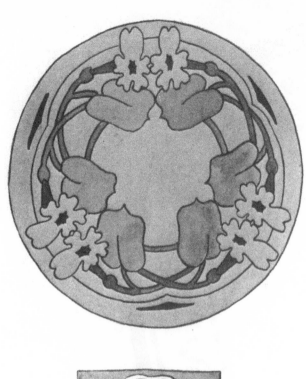

All 75

42

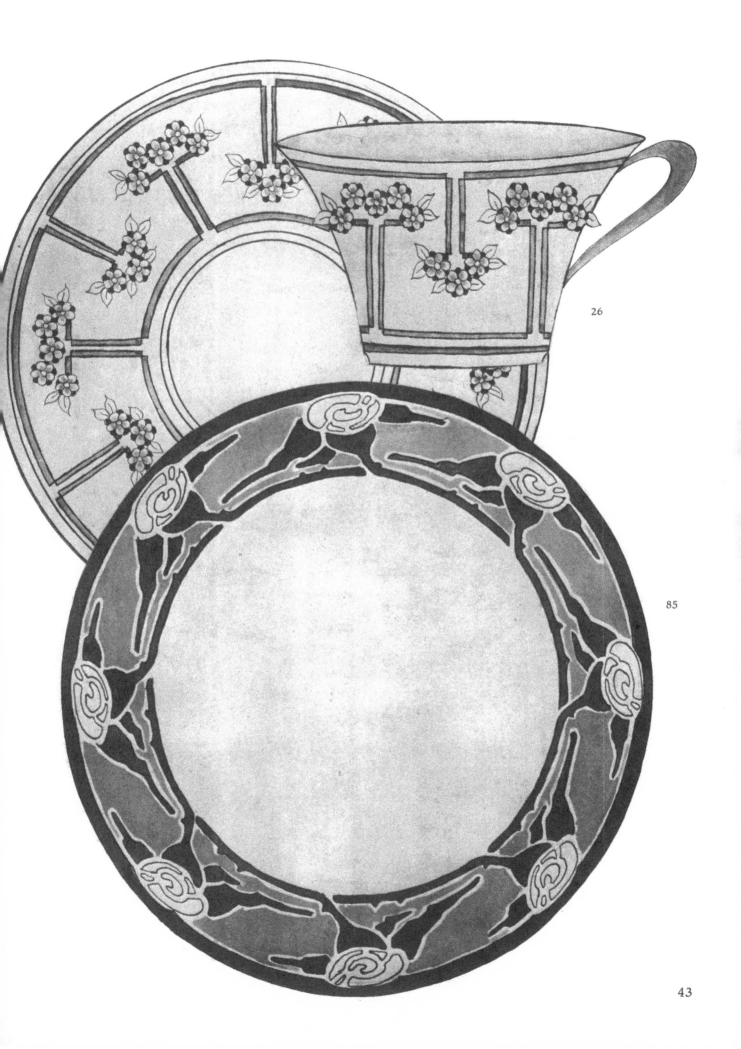

26

85

43

99

44

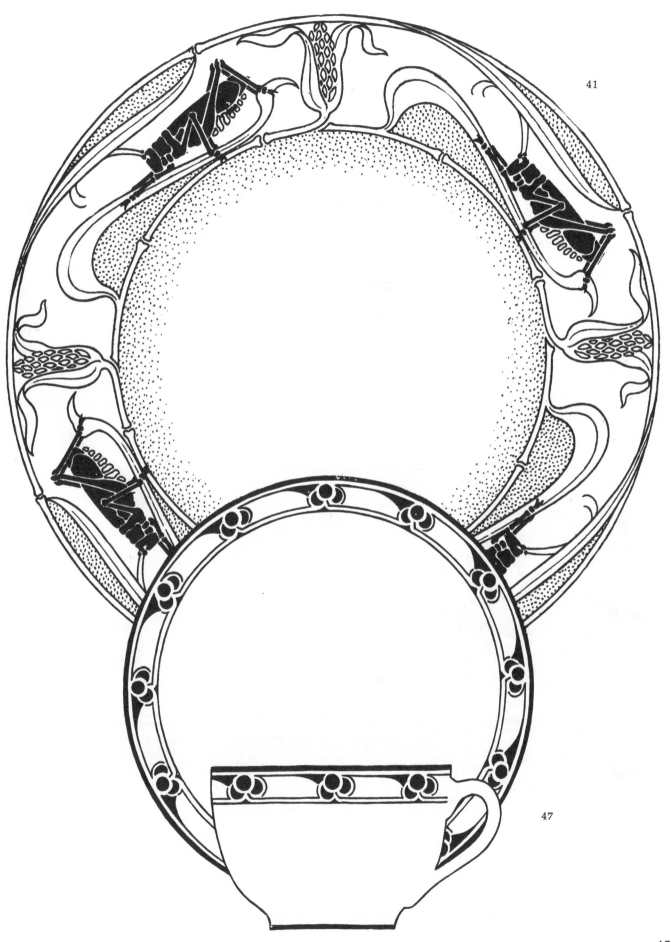

41

47

45

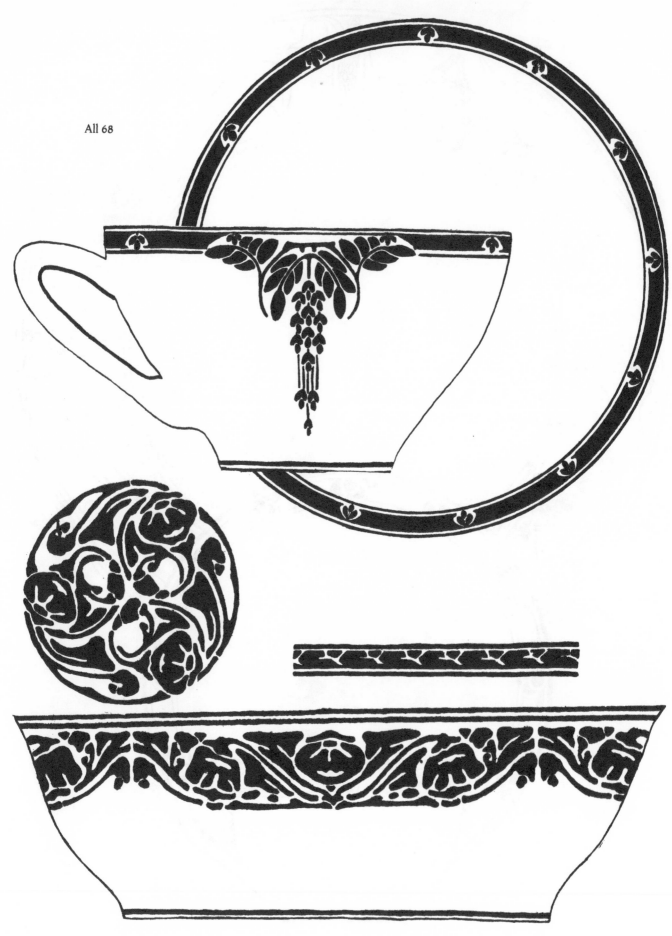

All 68

62

84

99

47

92

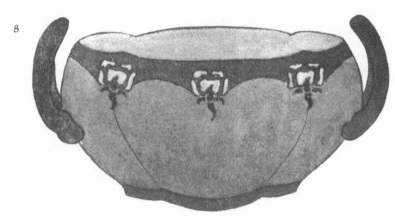

8

102

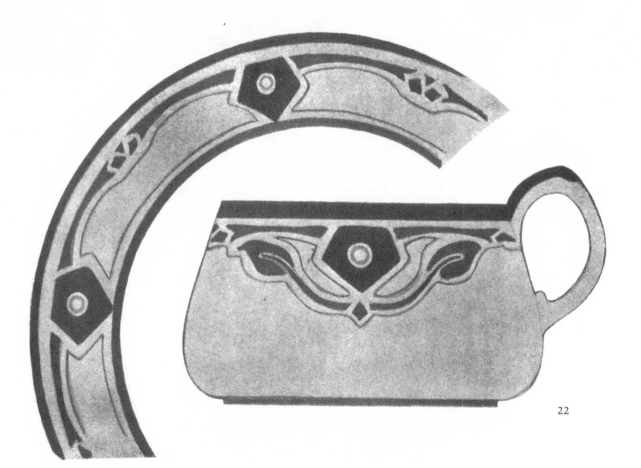

22

48

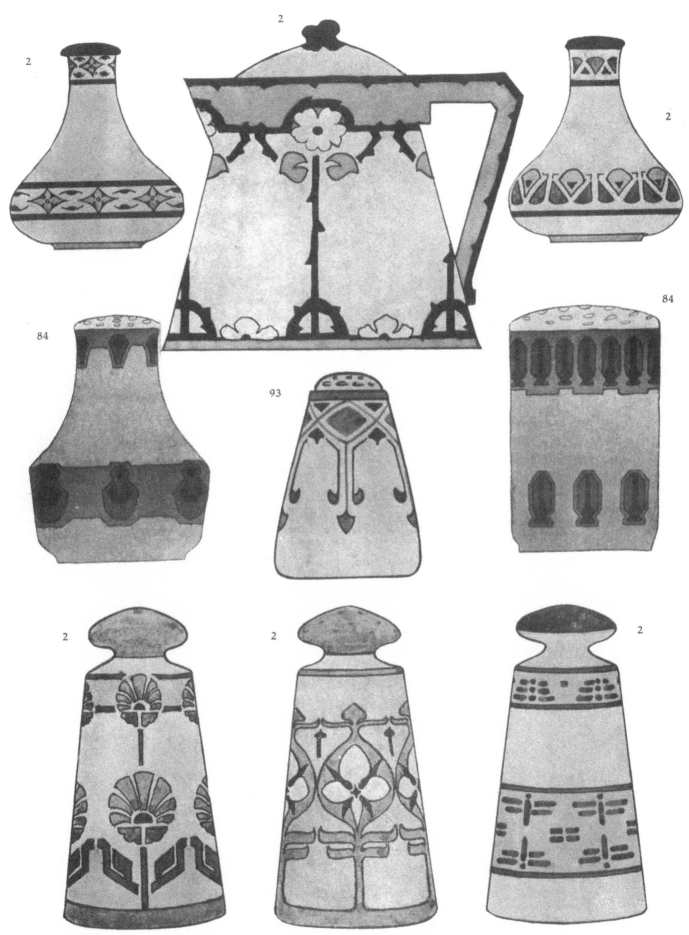

2

2

2

84

84

93

2

2

2

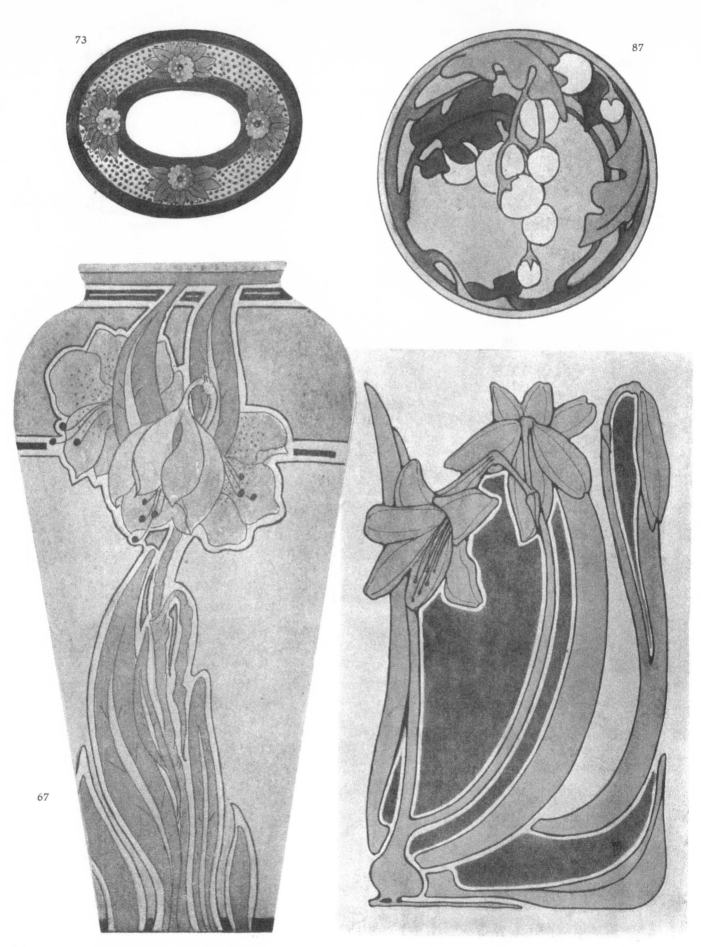

73

87

67

50

27

84

99

51

54

84

64

3

47

47

42

95

54

18

47

18

18

18

95

88

95

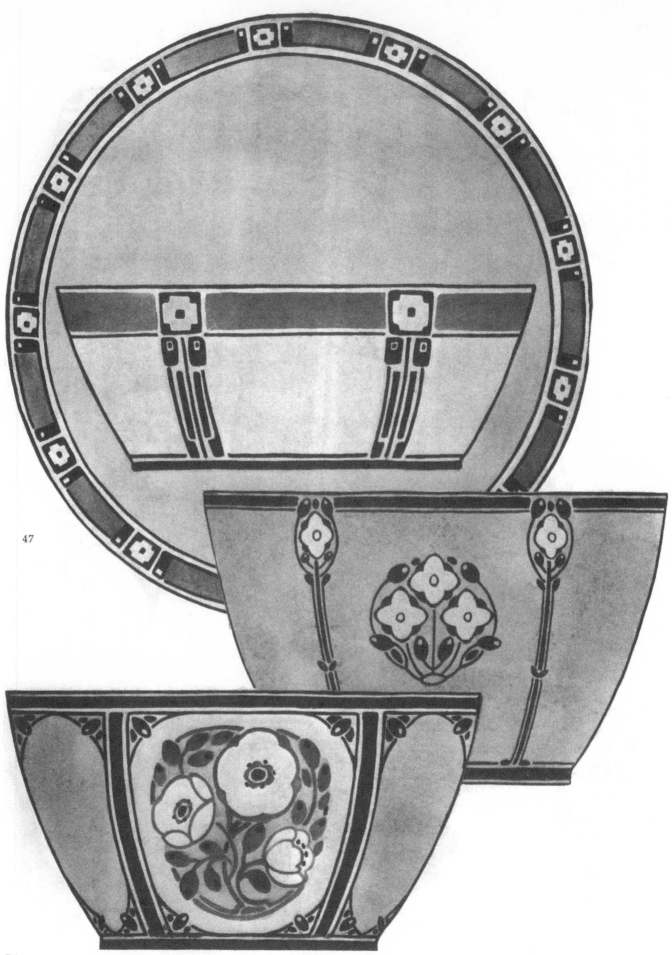

47

56

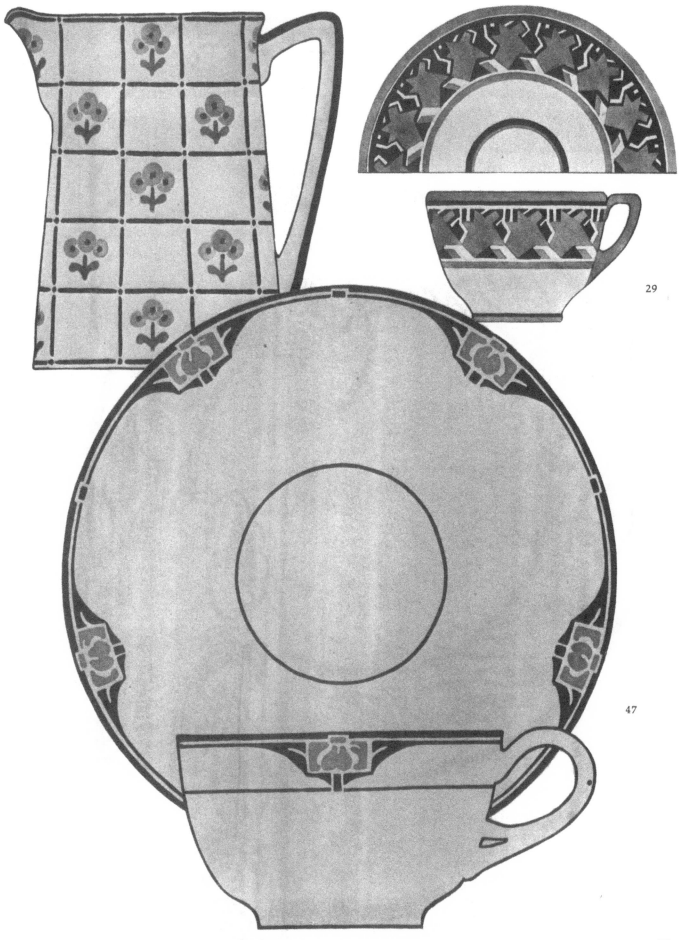

29

47

57

37

84

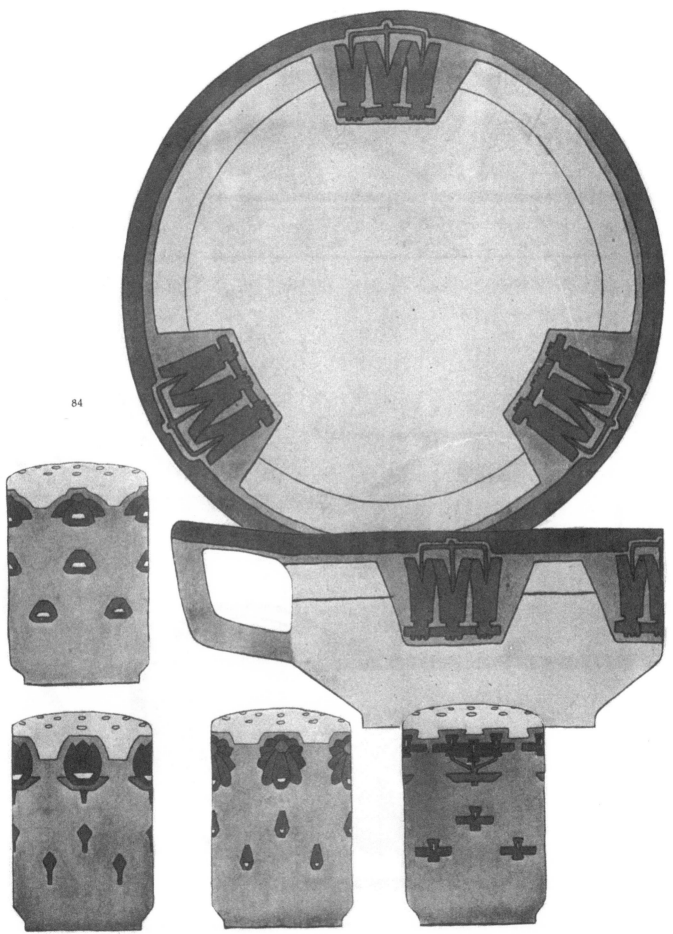

84

61

42

110

62

88

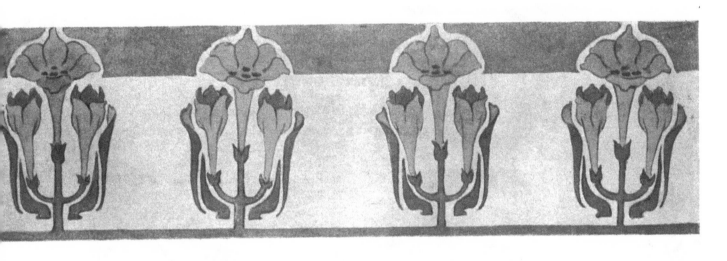

72

63

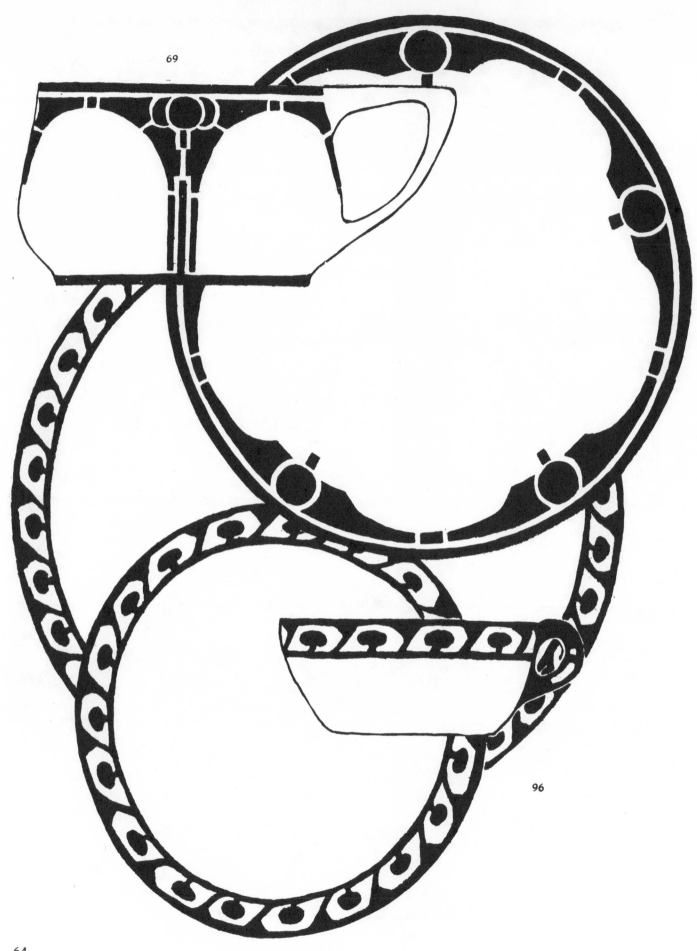

69

96

64

14

77

76

65

2

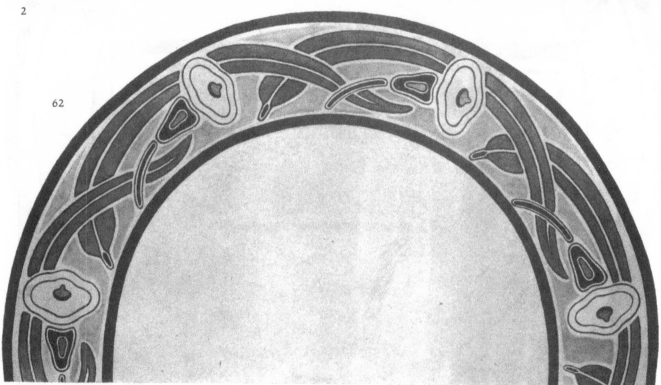

62

82

66

25

70

88

108

67

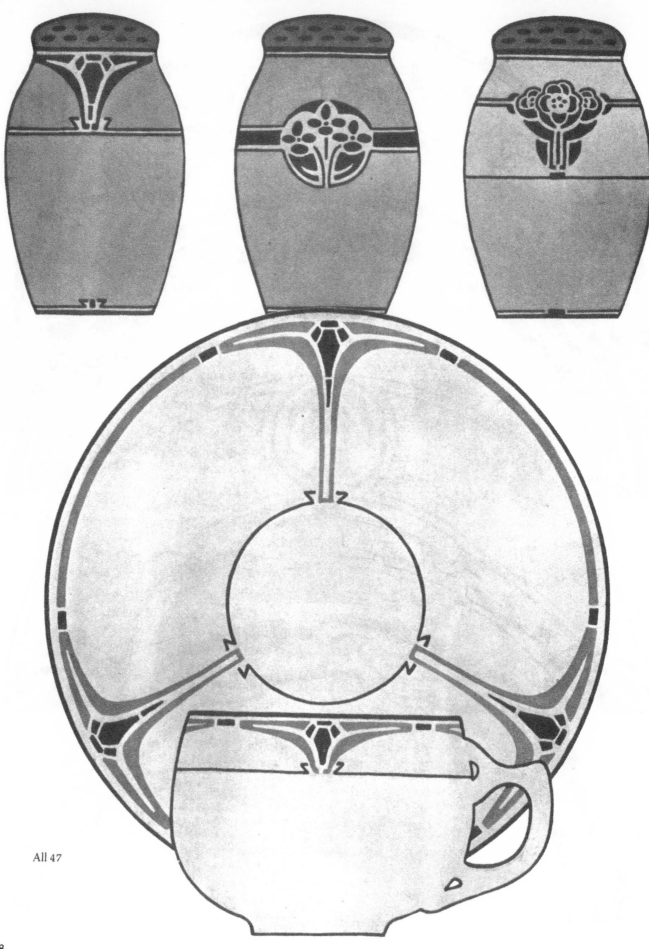

All 47

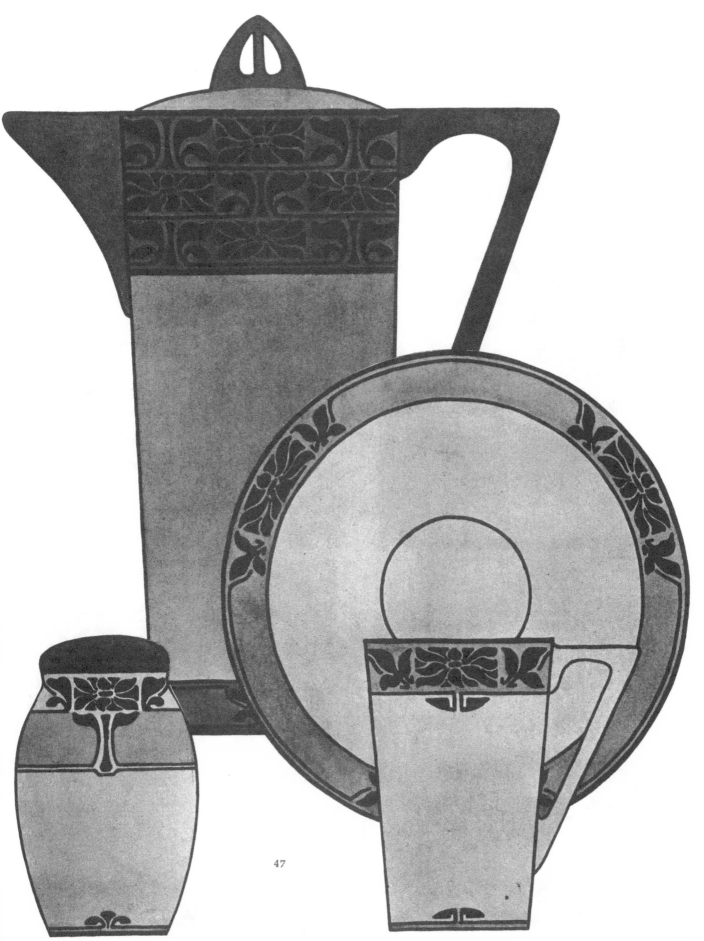

47

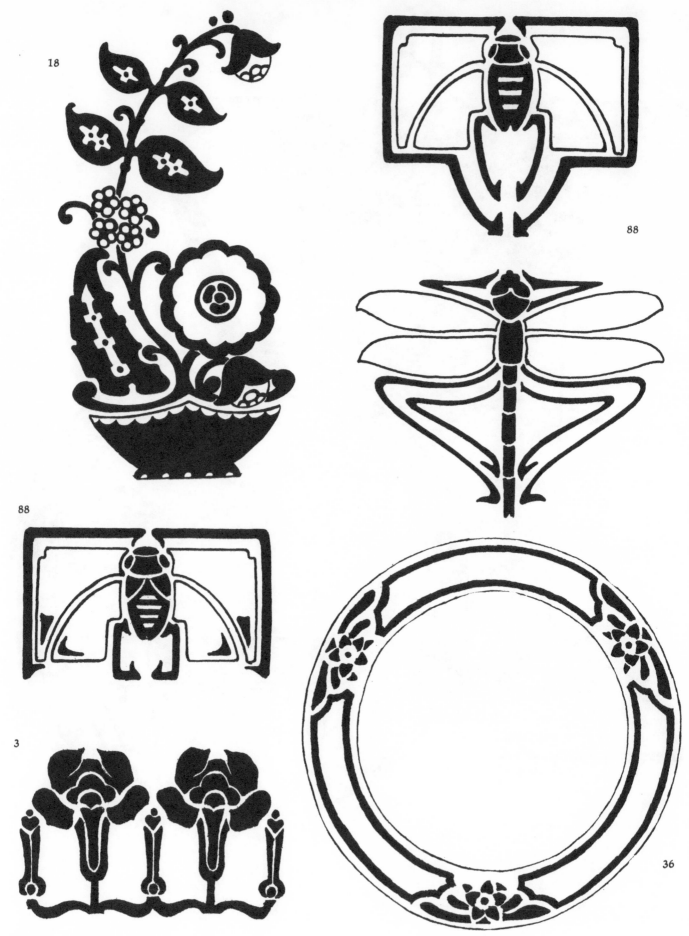

18

88

88

3

70

36

16

113

88

3

61

3

95

88

71

107

20

34

72

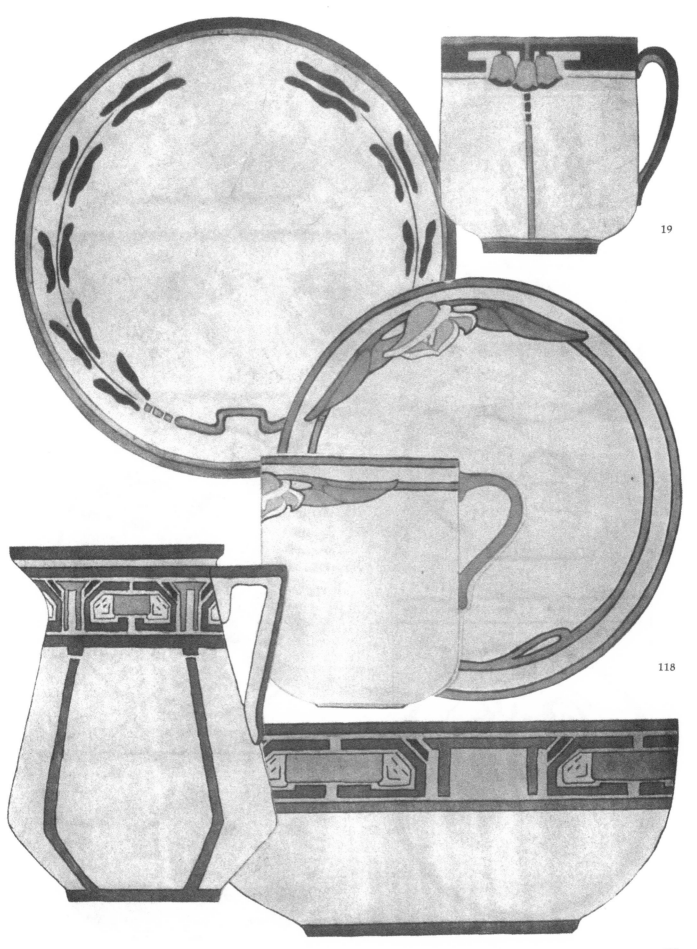

19

118

73

All 42

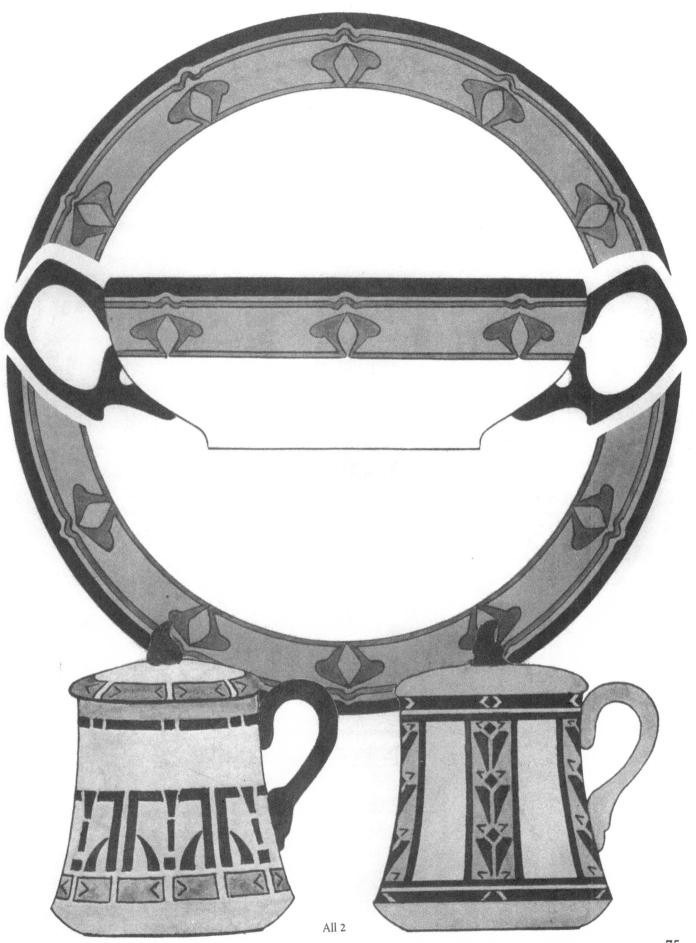

All 2

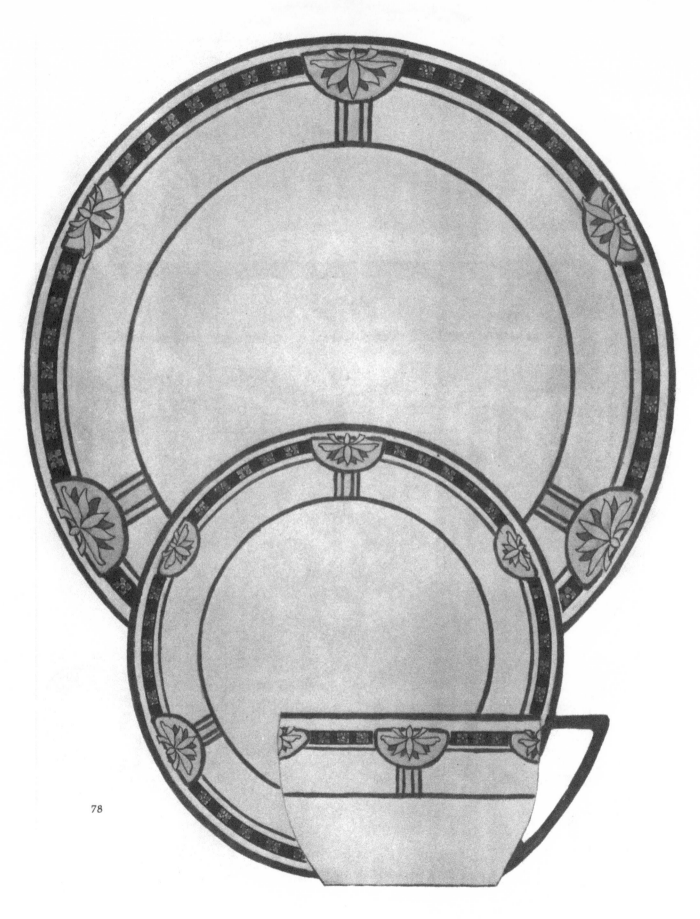

78

76

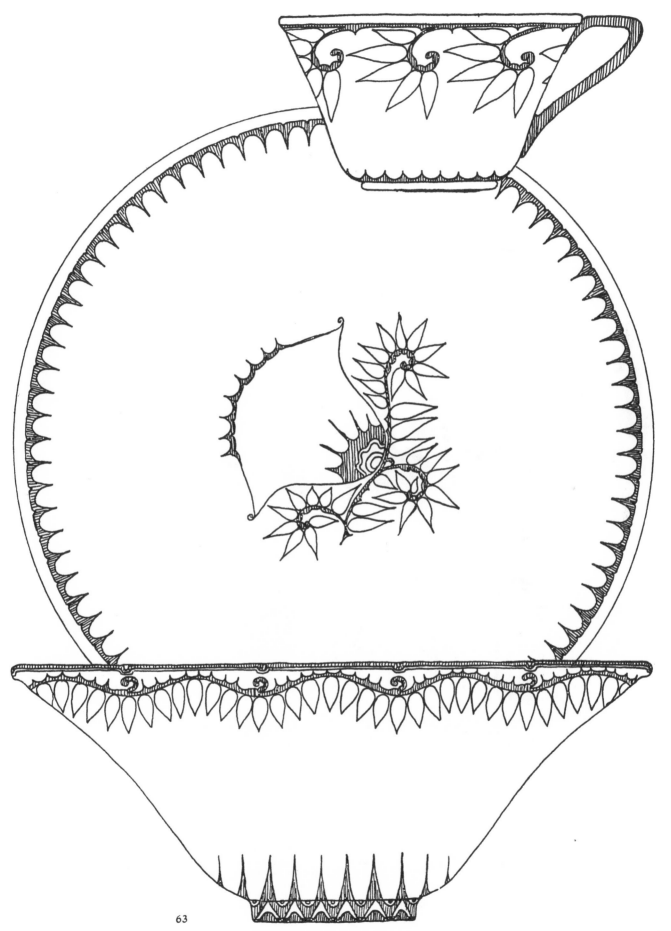

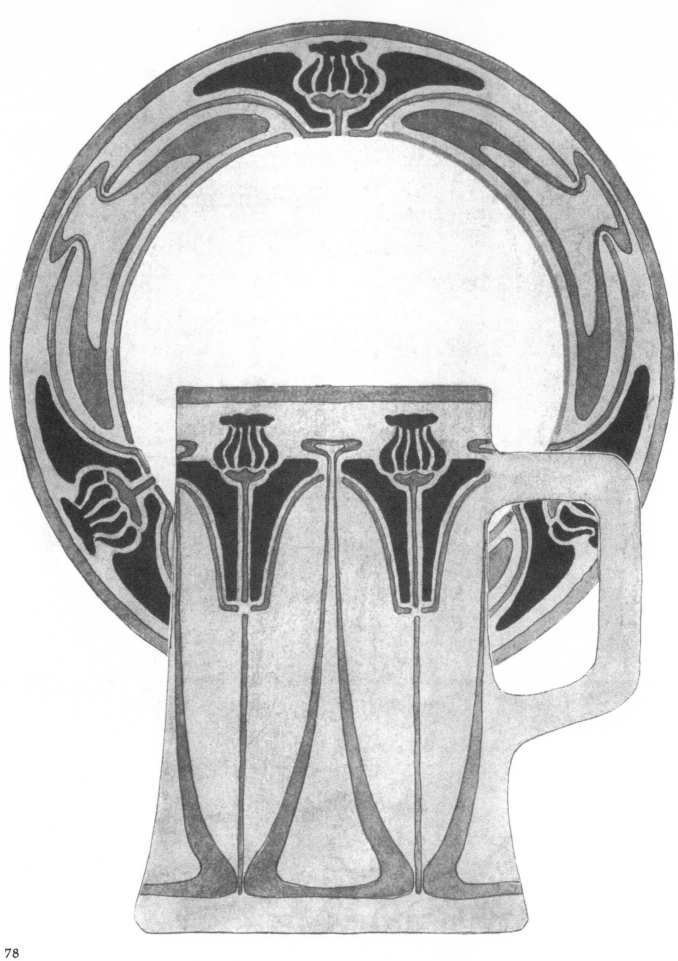

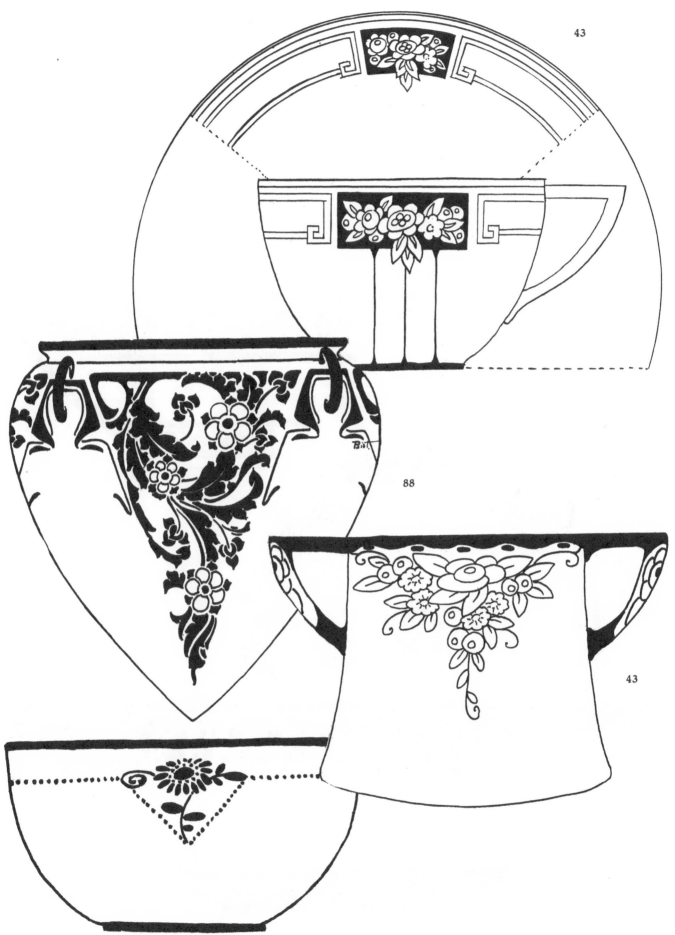

43

88

43

88

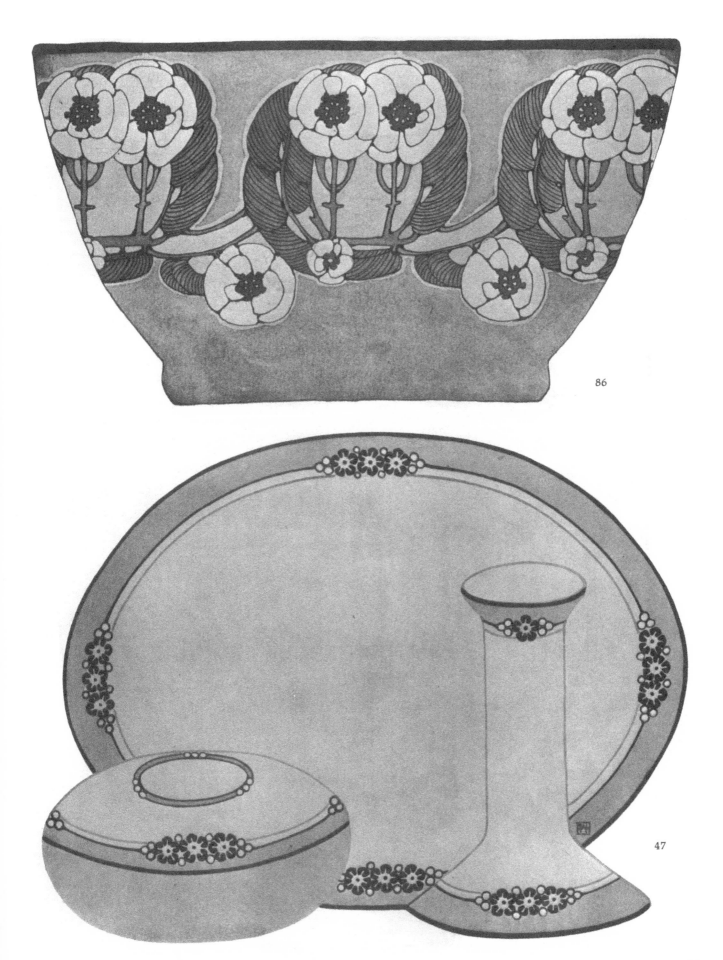

86

47

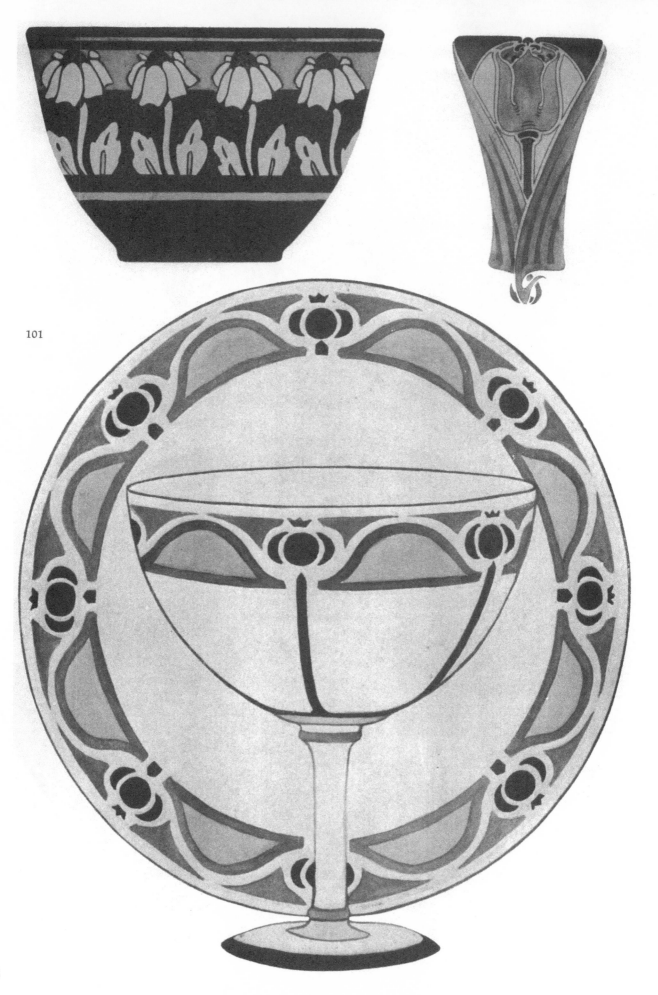

101

31

13

60

112

55

83

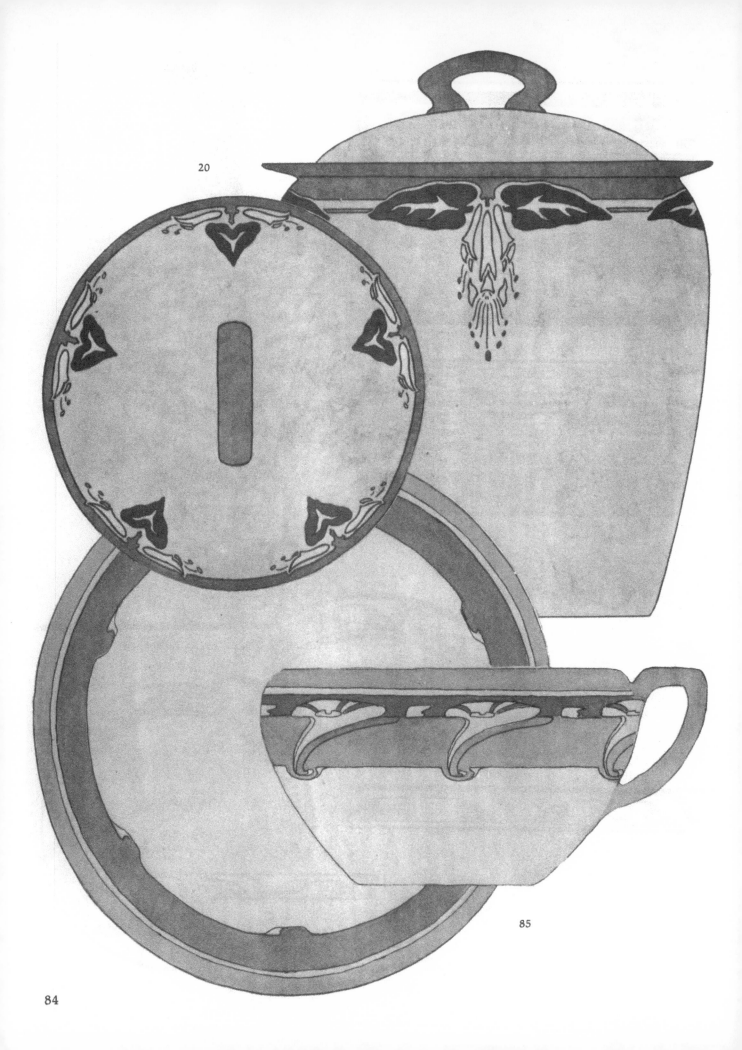

20

84

85

2

74

85

18

113

47

18

47

113

47

113

47

47

113

47

47

113

113

113

113

113

95

47

95

113

119

87

52

9

23

Francis Day

100

40

6

Evelyn Beachey – 1908

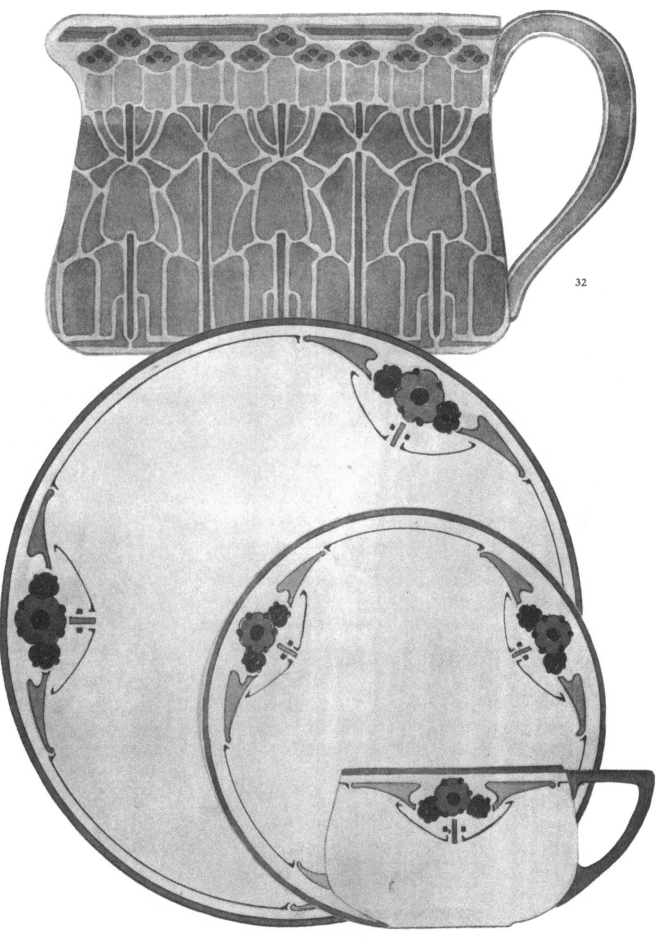

47

68

103

42

88

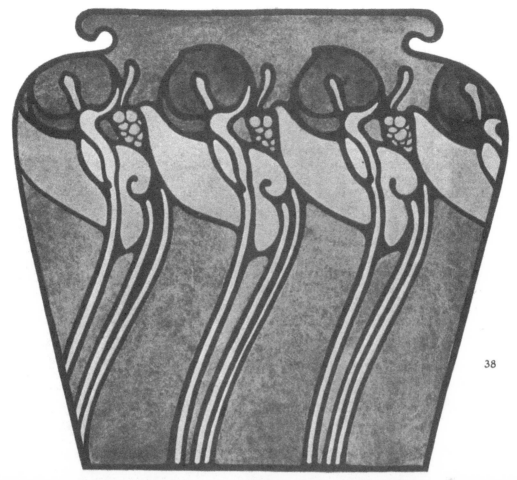

38

86

62

88

59

59

59

All 47

71

95

97

88

98

47

20

90

99

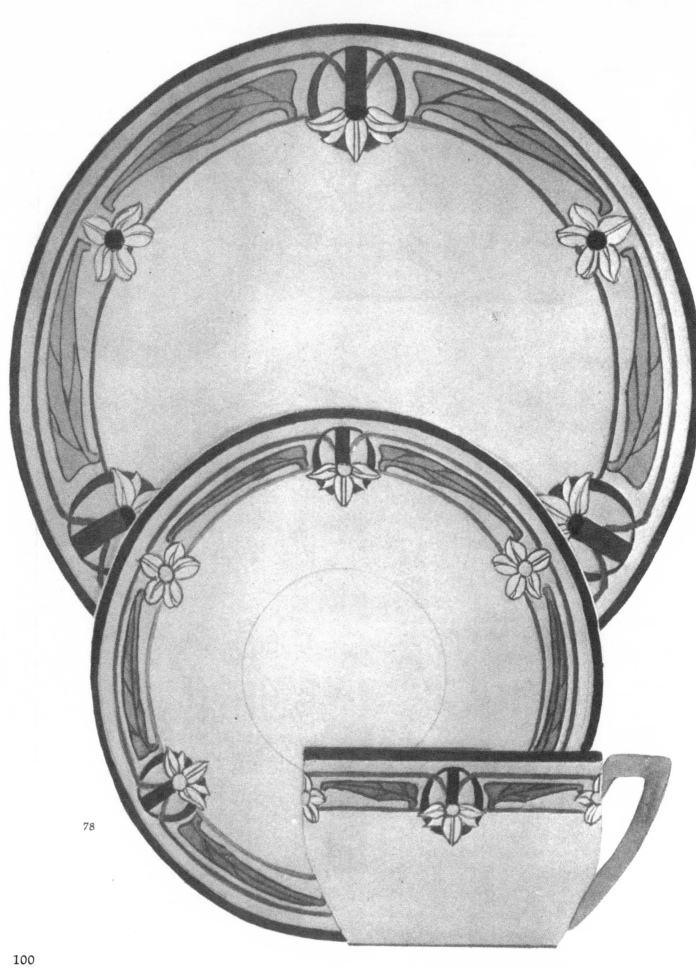

78

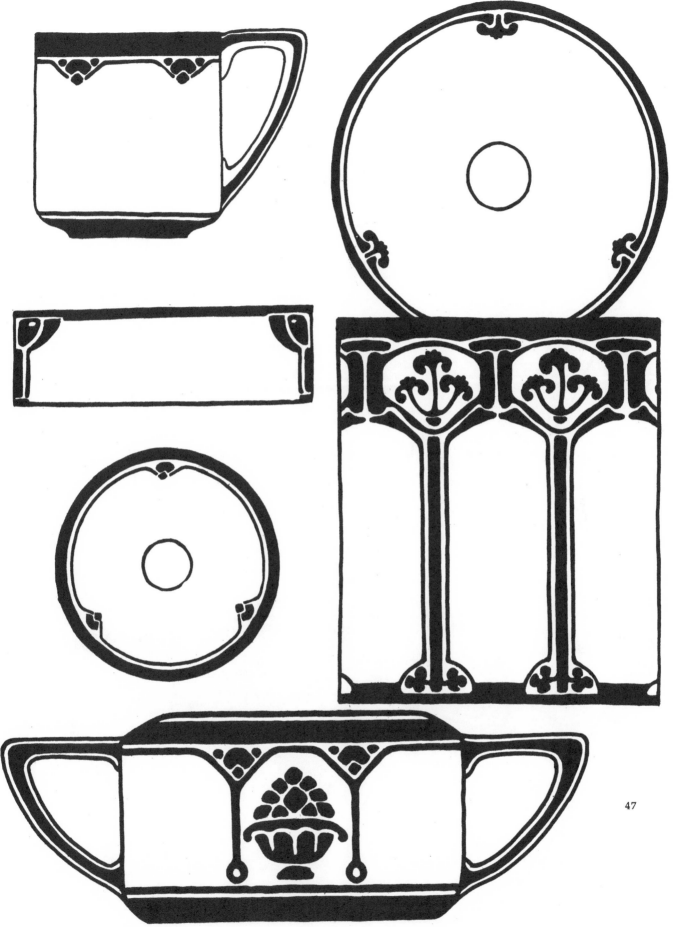

47

86

20

102

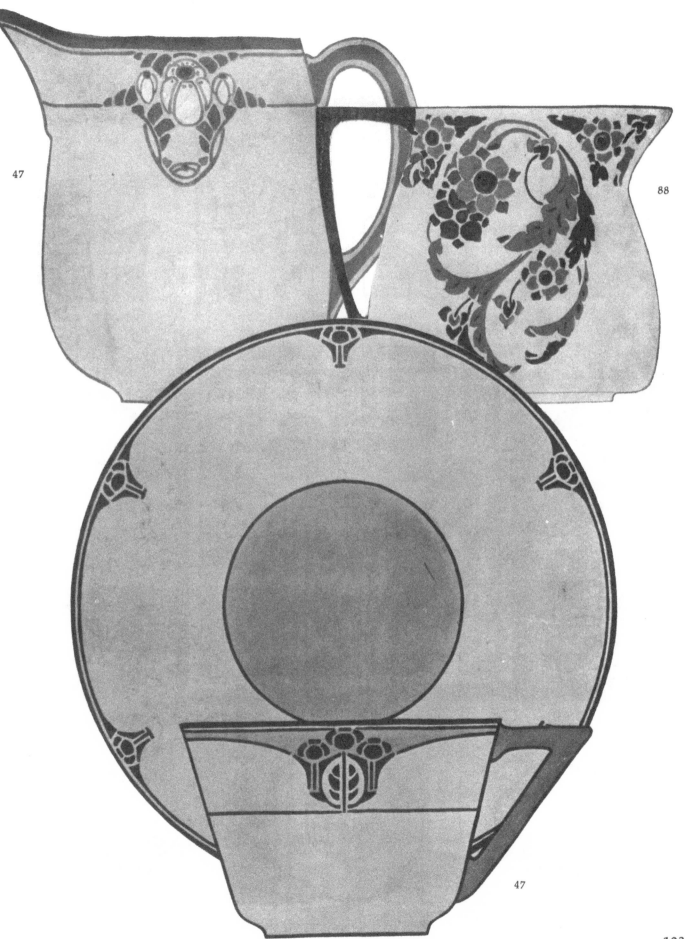

47

88

47

103

16

113

113

113

113

116

64

18

64

47

47

47

116

47

47

47

88

16

95

47

47

95

105

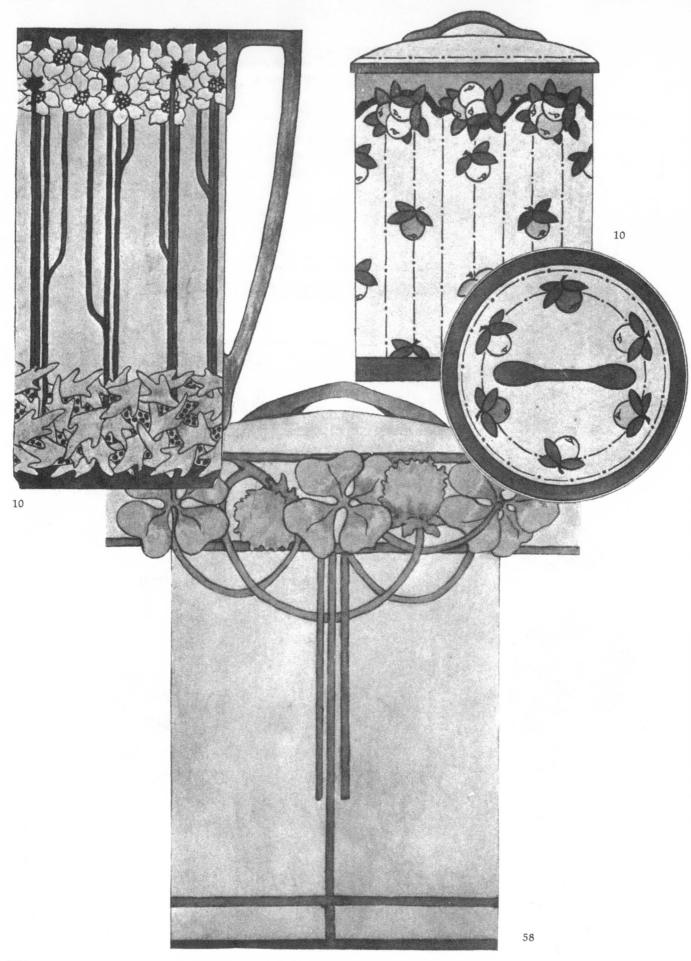

10

10

58

106

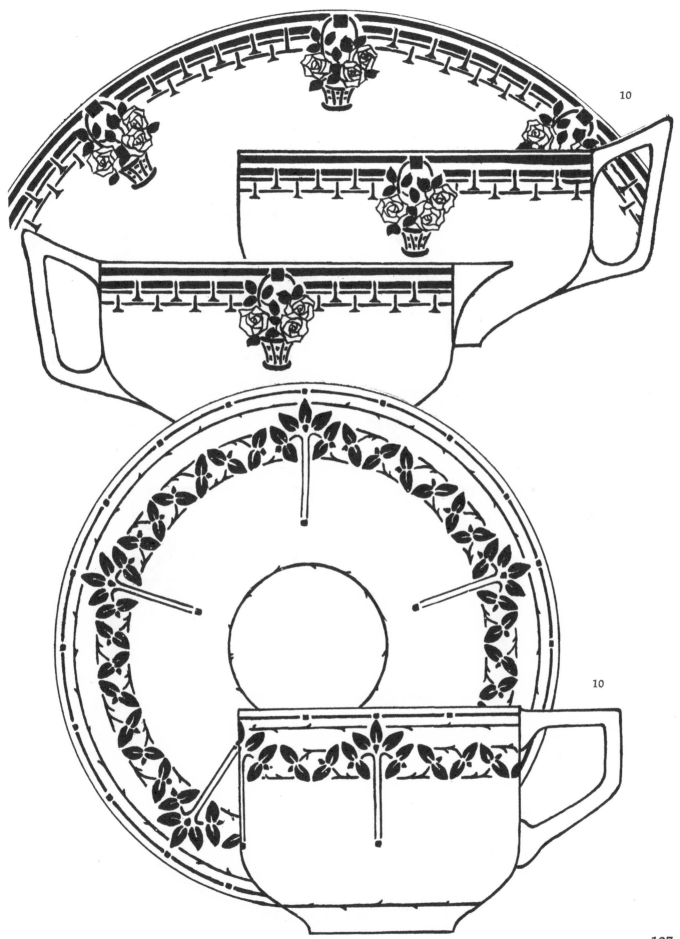

10

10

107

42

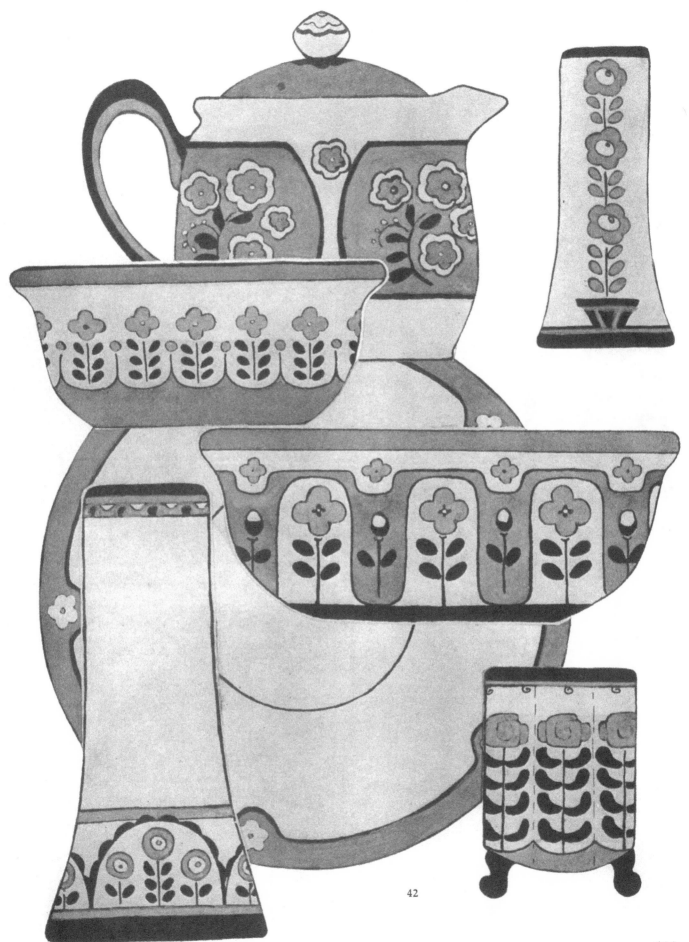

42

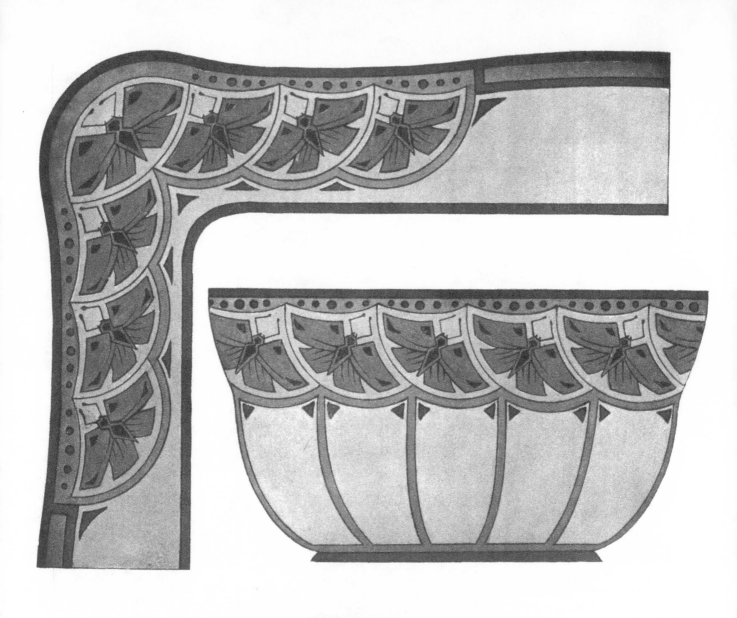

98

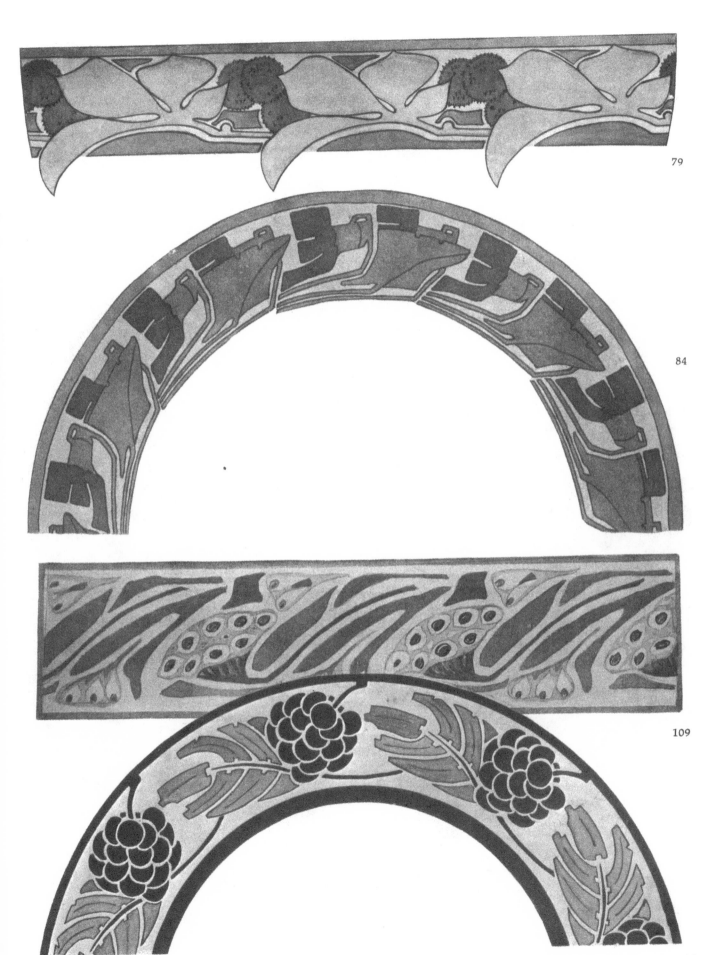

79

84

109

111

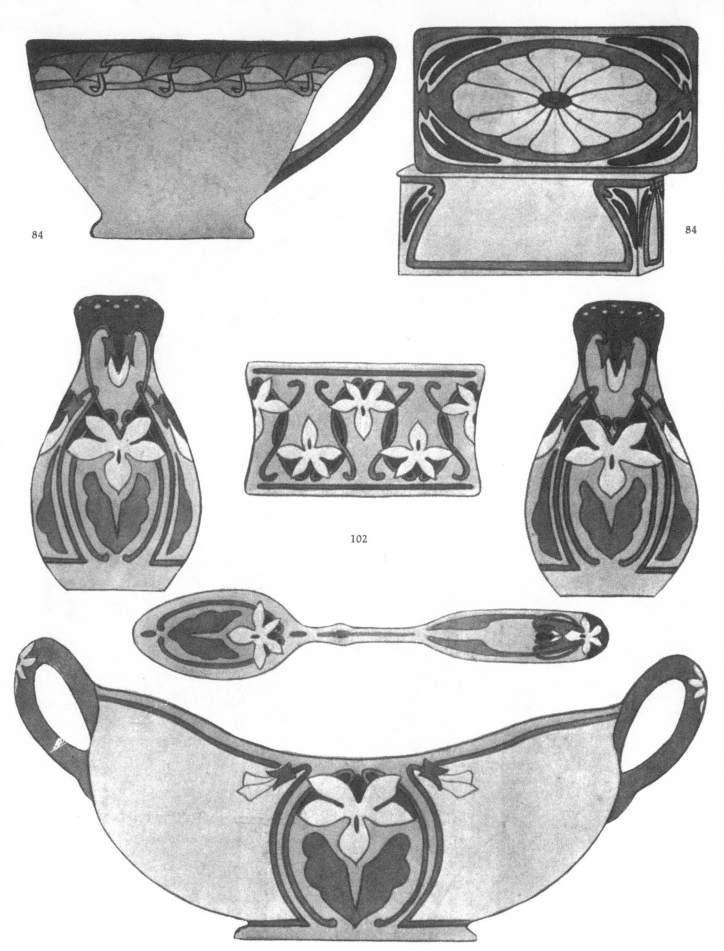

84

84

102

112

120

18

42

66

110

102

2

115

47

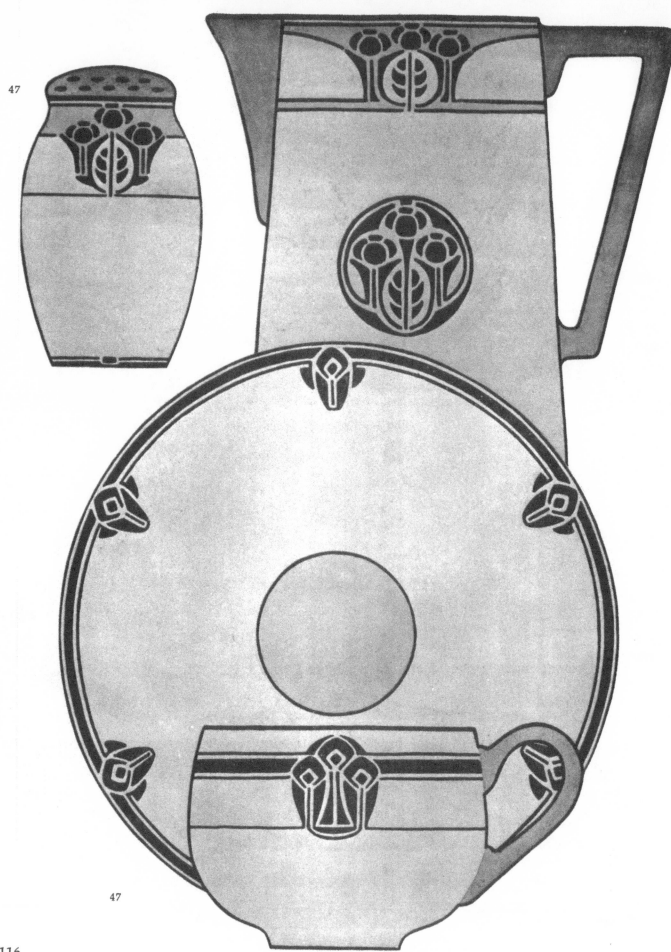

47

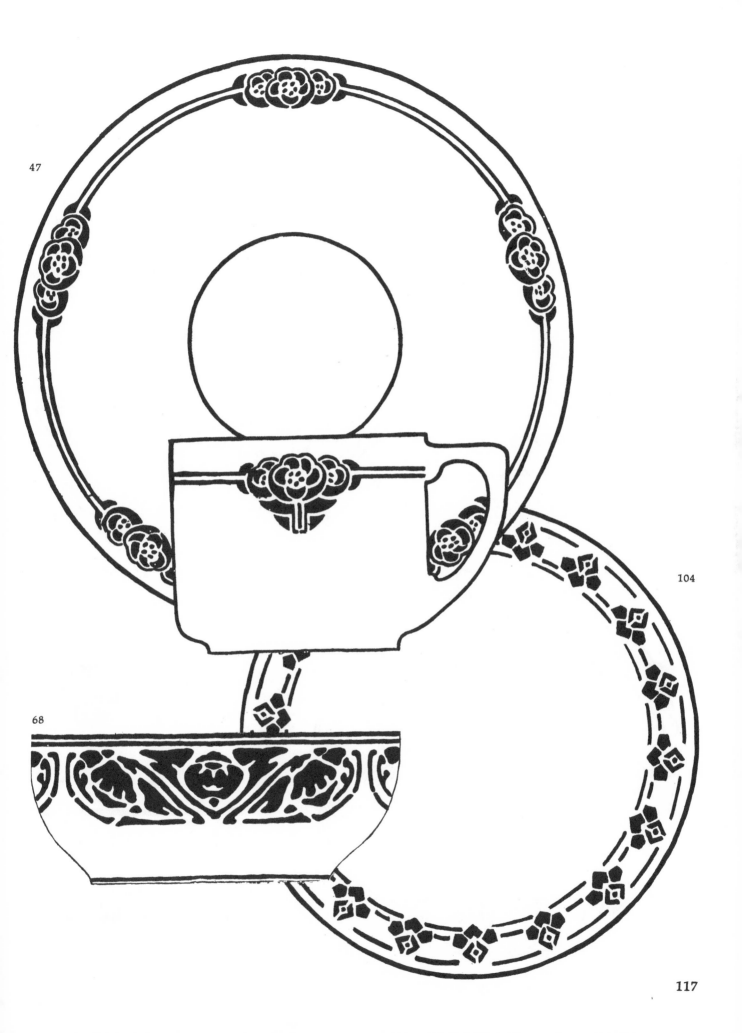

47

104

68

117

22

88

16

38

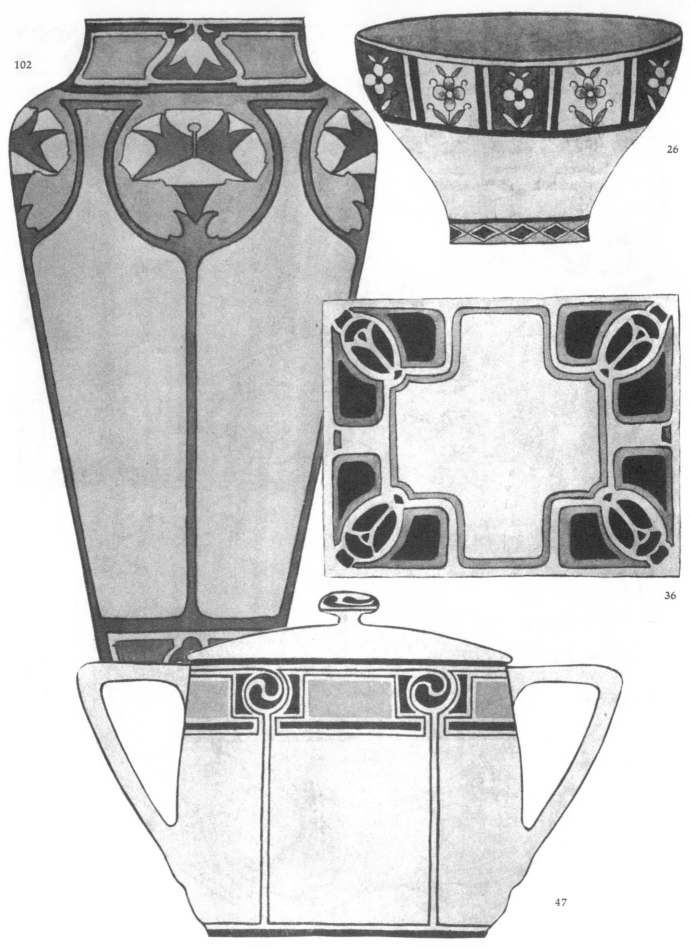

102

26

36

47

120

26

53

88

51

Henrietta Barclay Paint

121